The Spoke Art
SF Annual

2018

Table of Contents

Introduction

Dasha Matsuura

It's hard to believe 2018 is already coming to a close. We've had an incredibly exciting (and busy) year filled with dynamic group shows, incredible solo exhibitions featuring long-time artists returning to the gallery with new work as well as fresh faces showing with us for the first time.

The year started off with two artists who have been part of the Spoke family since the beginning, *Matt and Miles Ritchie*. It was particularly special for us to have this father and son duo at the gallery for *Pop Perspective* as we've watched both of them grow as artists and to get to see such an amazing intergenerational love for all things pop culture.

In February I was thrilled to curate a group exhibition featuring tattoo artists from around the world. *FLASH* is a show I've wanted to do for a very long time and I felt incredibly honored to work with so many talented artists. Special thanks to *Stephanie Brown*, *Mike Davis* and *Jeery* for turning the gallery into a tattoo shop for opening weekend!

Just in time for Spring, we welcomed long-time friend of the gallery *Tatiana Suarez* for her first solo show with us. The lovely work in *Nymphaea* was the perfect welcome to warmer weather and exciting news of Tati's growing family. Congratulations on your most ambitious art project yet!

We kicked it into high gear in April for rock poster legend *Chuck Sperry's* solo show *Heaven of Many a Tangled Hue*. Legions of dedicated collectors camped out in front of the gallery to get their hands on his masterfully printed pieces. A heartfelt thank you to everyone who travelled to see the show and of course to Chuck, who is one of the hardest working and kindest artists around.

With only a few group shows on the books for the year, I couldn't wait for *12 x 12* in May. Format exhibitions are always exhilarating in that we don't know what subject matter, media or composition artists will find inspiring for their contributions. After a successful run in San Francisco, we took the show on the road to Chicago in the Fall.

June brought us the humorous and poignant work of *Scott Listfield*. The newly relocated Los Angeles-based painter, created a body of succinctly Bay Area works that poked at our hometown's obsession with future tech. We can't wait for Scott's forthcoming book *Astronaut*, debuting at the end of 2018.

The following month, we welcomed **David Welker** back to San Francisco for his second sold out solo exhibition. This incredibly detailed work explored some of David's longstanding themes like architecture and nature while also delving more into abstracted forms. We are excited to see where he'll go next!

August and September brought us two solo exhibitions by two of our favorite local painters, **Nadezda** and **Helice Wen**. Both artists are fixtures of the local arts community and share an affinity for expressive oil painting. Nadezda plunged us into her world filled with dark and mysterious fairytales, while Helice invited us into her bright and intimate tableaus. In addition to being talented painters, both artists also direct and orchestrate elaborate photoshoots that serve as source material and inspiration for their paintings. It was inspiring to get to peek behind the curtain and see their intimate processes.

We have been big fans of **Amy Sol's** work for a long time and are elated that she not only moved to the Bay Area this year, but also gave us a gorgeous show. She has continued to grow not only as a painter but as an exceptional sculptor. I can't wait to see what new techniques she incorporates next into her work.

Social media can feel like a blessing and curse with constantly shifting and evolving platforms and algorithms. **Paintguide** is definitely a bright spot, serving as a communal meeting point to share inspiration and new work. When they approached us about collaborating on a show, we jumped at the chance! It was great to connect with a whole new set of international artists and incorporate a few of our familiar favorites.

A heartfelt thank you to our incredible Spoke team, the talented artists who have entrusted us with the distinct honor of showing their work and our dedicated fans and collectors. We truly couldn't do this without each and every one of you. We are looking forward to a bustling 2019 with more traveling shows, art fairs and pop ups that we can't wait to share with you.

Dasha Matsuura,
Director, San Francisco

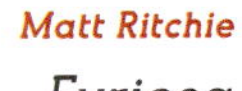

Matt Ritchie
Furiosa
wood, acrylic paint,
felt, plexiglass
8˝ x 10˝ (2017)

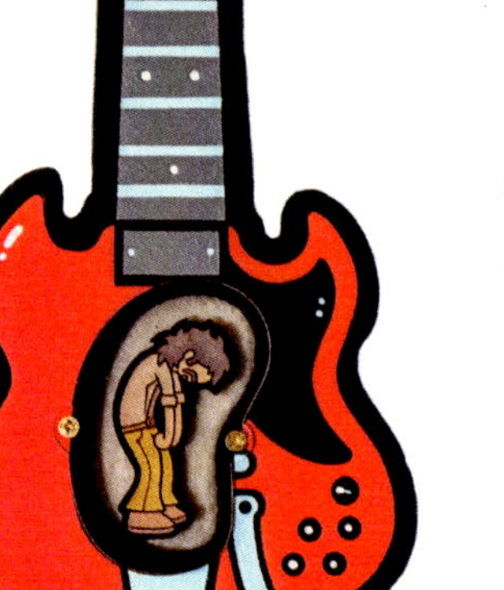

Matt Ritchie
Zappa
wood, paper, markers,
acrylic paint, felt, plexiglass
7˝ x 3¾˝ (2017)

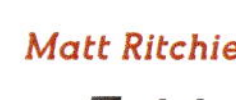

Matt Ritchie
Zelda
wood, paper, markers,
acrylic paint, felt, plexiglass
11¼˝ x 6˝ (2017)

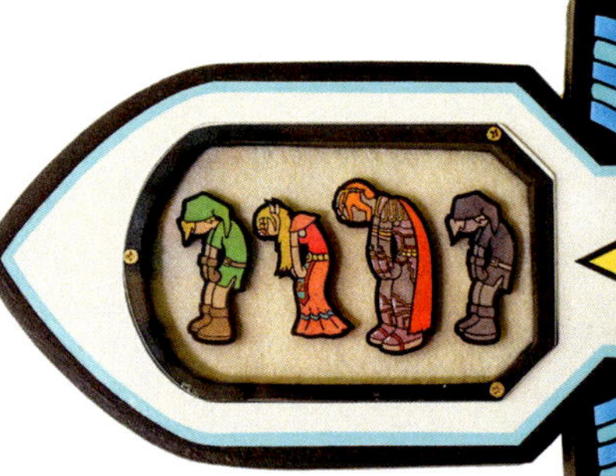

Matt Ritchie
Battlestar Viper
wood, paper, markers,
acrylic paint, plexiglass, felt
9˝ x 4˝ (2017)

Matt Ritchie
Horror Drop #12 (Jason)
wood, acrylic paint, plexiglass, felt
7˝ x 4˝ (2017)

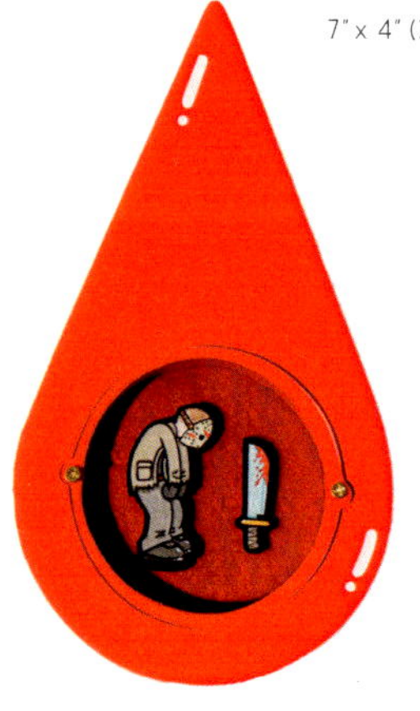

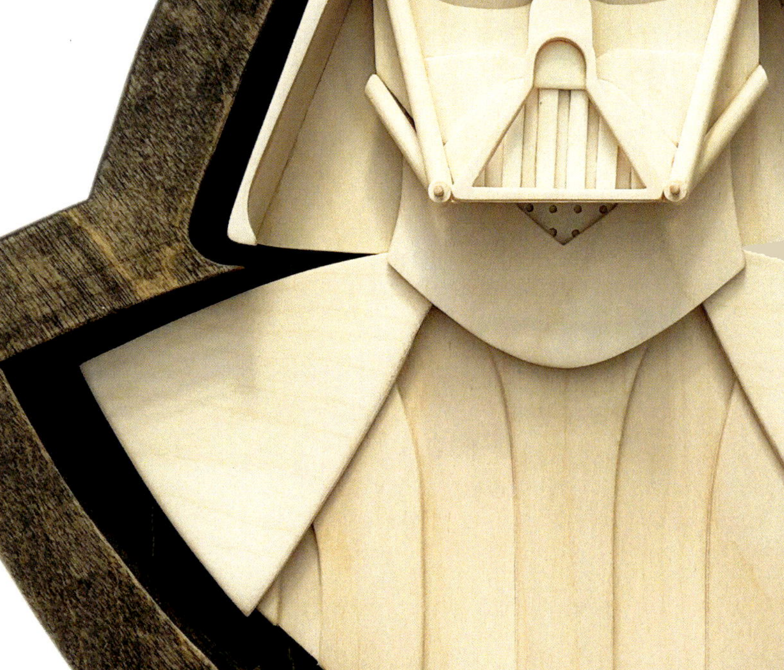

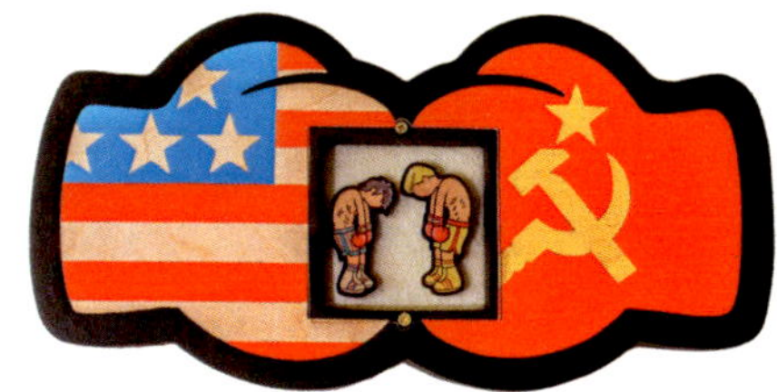

Matt Ritchie
Rocky 4
wood, paper, markers,
acrylic paint, felt, plexiglass
10" x 5" (2017)

Pop Perspective

Matt Ritchie & Miles Ritchie

**January 6–27
2018**

Miles Ritchie
Vader
wood
12" x 13" (2017)

SPOKE SF presents *Pop Perspective*, a dual artist exhibition featuring new work by *Matt & Miles Ritchie*. For their debut exhibition together, this father and son duo has created a fun and affordable pop culture experience featuring hand cut and painted wooden sculptures and paintings complimenting their two distinct artistic styles. Ranging from the Avengers to Zelda, Pop Perspective is a comprehensive pop culture survey from the perspective of two different generations.

Sharing a mutual love for comics, film, TV, music, video games and everything pop, Matt & Miles Ritchie distill their favorite characters and icons into crisply crafted and dimensional pieces.

Matt Ritchie's colorful painted wood pieces explore individual characters and their iconic accouterments, concentrating on the immediately recognizable essentials. His slump series is "*an exhausted look at exhausted pop,*" celebrating the artist's deep love for pop culture & commenting on the ubiquitous over saturation of each franchise.

Where his Dad's perspective is steeped in decades of fandom, Miles Ritchie is presenting beloved characters with fresh eyes. Simplifying and refining many of the same characters, the younger Ritchie takes a more minimal approach to rendering his "Pop Ply Portraits" using only natural wood and shadow.

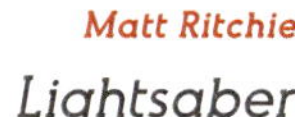

Matt Ritchie
Lightsaber
wood, paper, markers,
acrylic paint, felt, plexiglass
17½" x 5½" (2017)

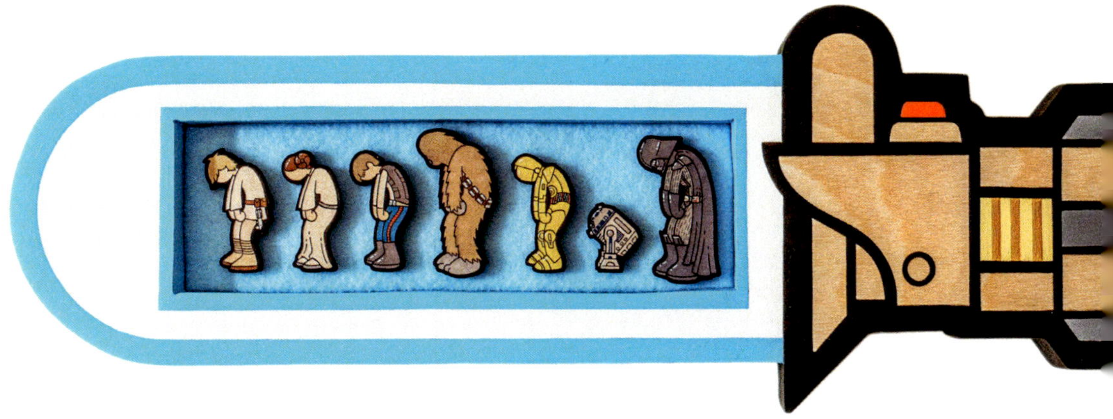

CENTER:

Miles Ritchie
Pennywise
wood
10˝ x 12½˝ (2017)

Matt Ritchie
Horror Drops #1–13
wood, acrylic paint, plexiglass, felt
7˝ x 4˝ (2017)

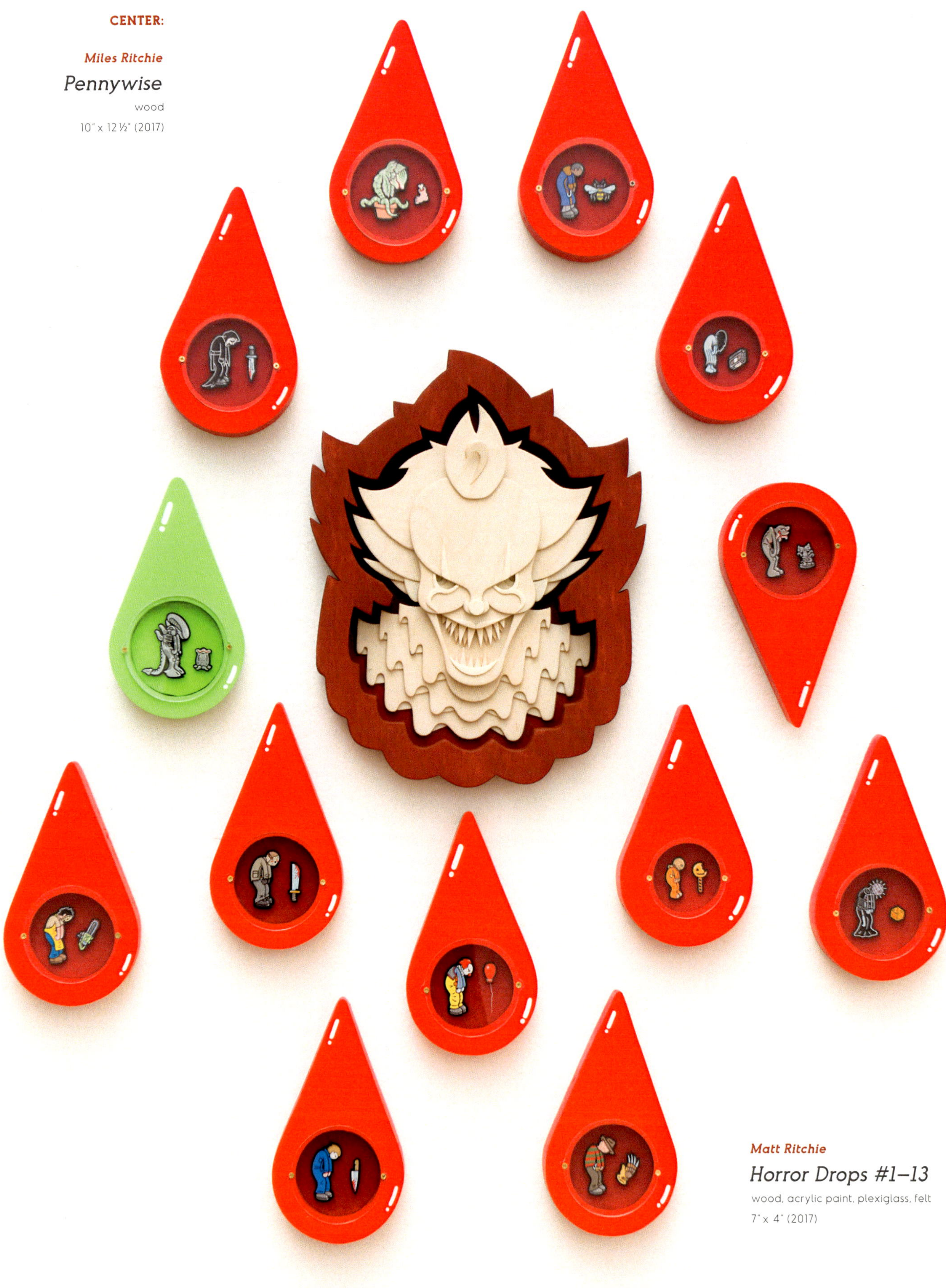

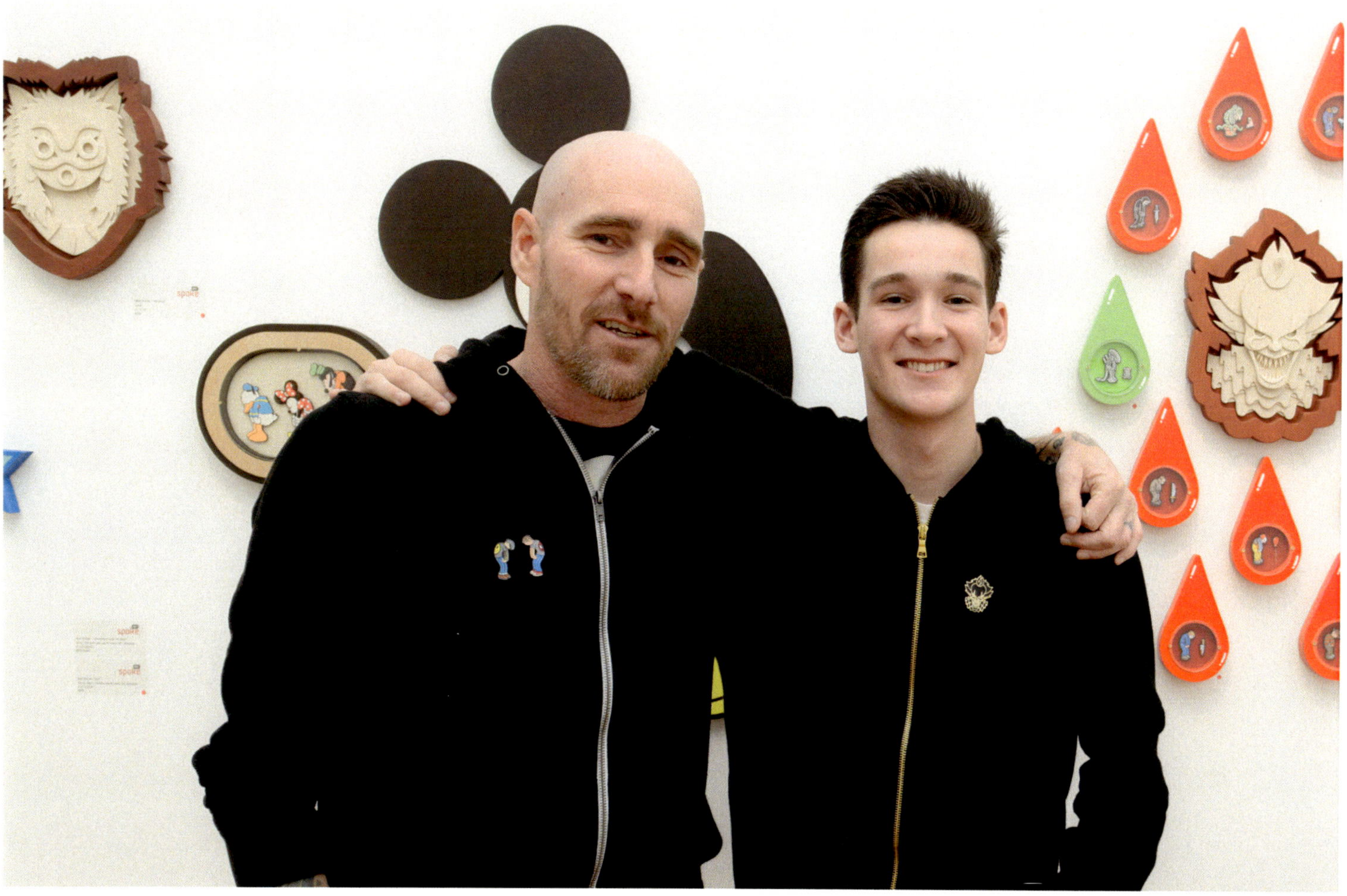

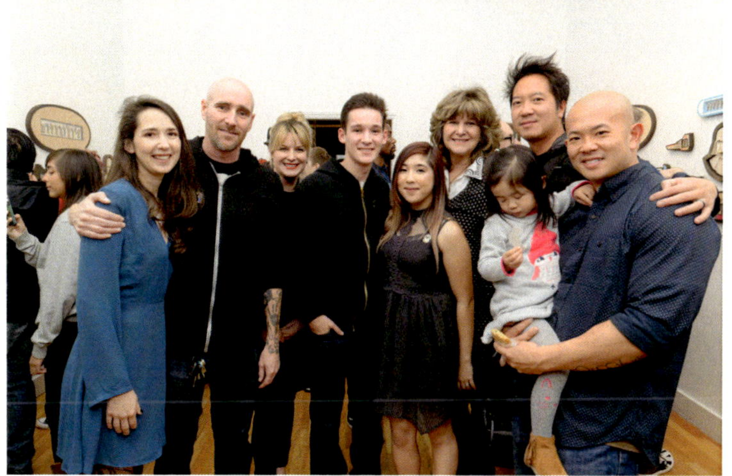
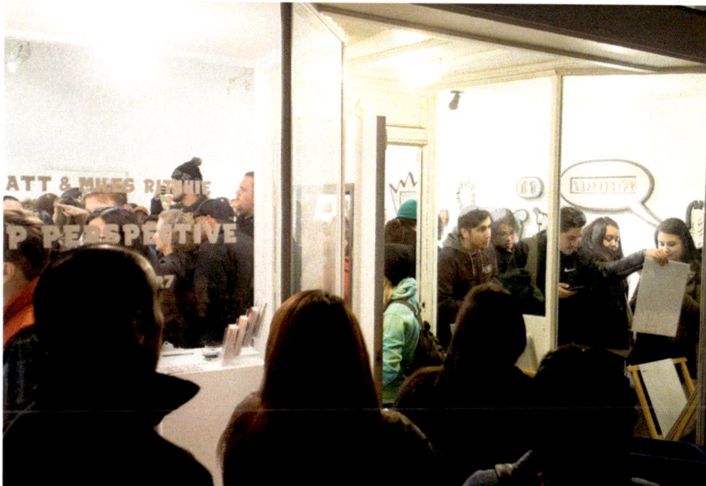
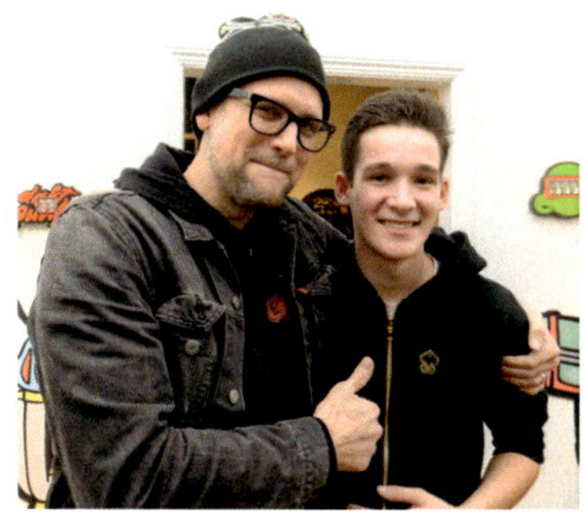
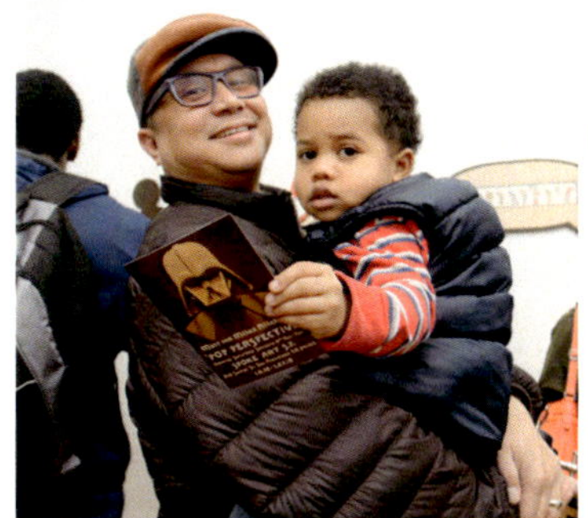
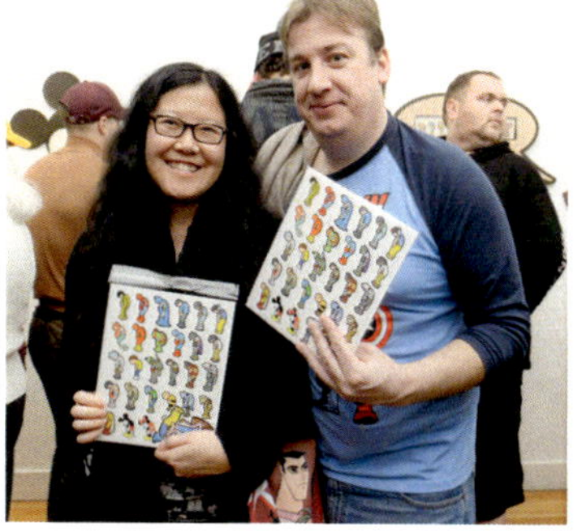
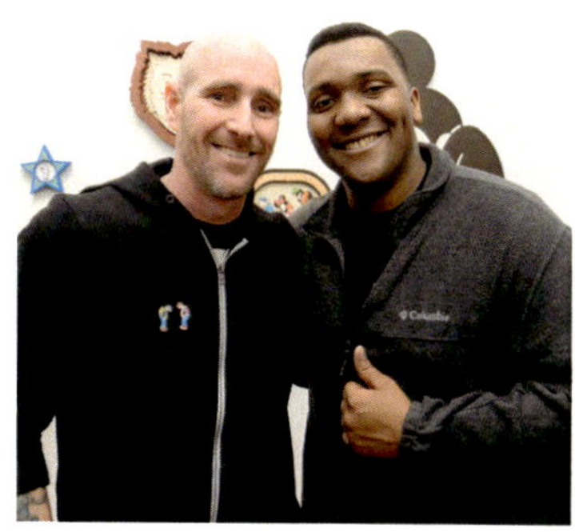

Opening Reception
PHOTOS: Shaun Roberts

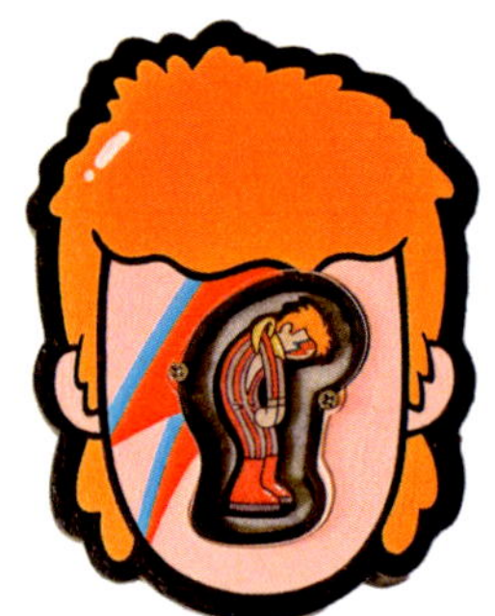

A.

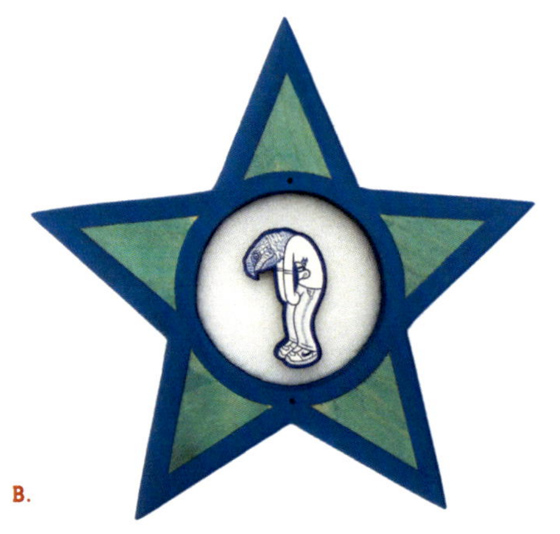

B.

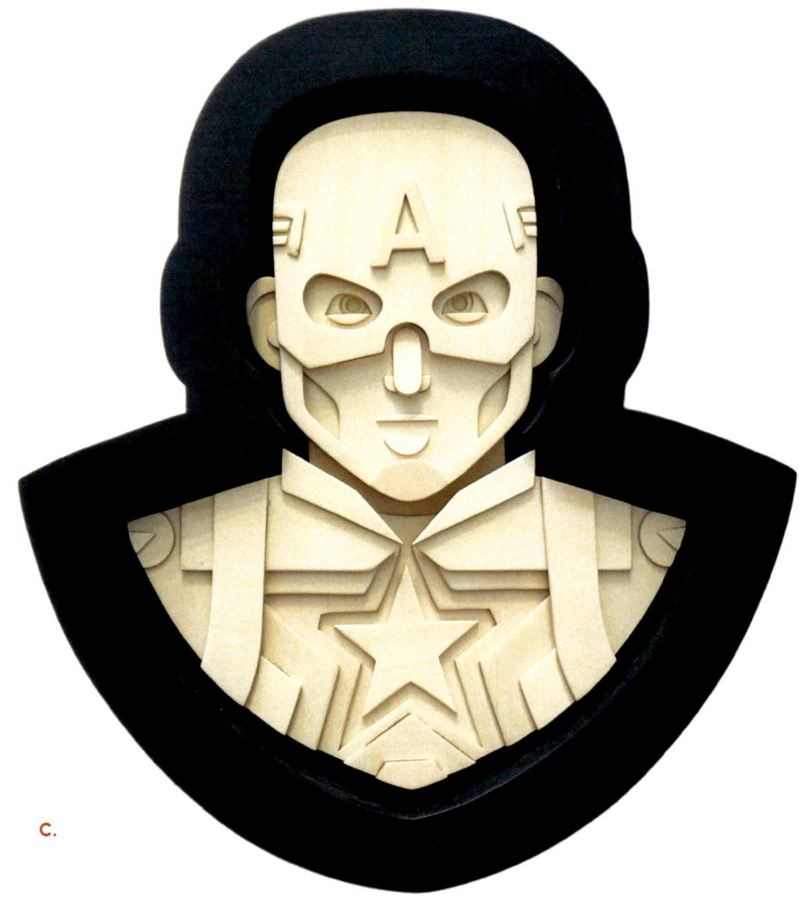

C.

A. *Matt Ritchie*

Starman

wood, markers, paper,
acrylic paint, plexiglass, felt
8¾" x 5½" (2017)

B. *Matt Ritchie*

Anthropomorphic All-Stars (Turtle)

wood, ball point pen,
acrylic paint, plexiglass, felt
8" x 8" (2017)

C. *Miles Ritchie*

Captain

wood
10½" x 11½" (2017)

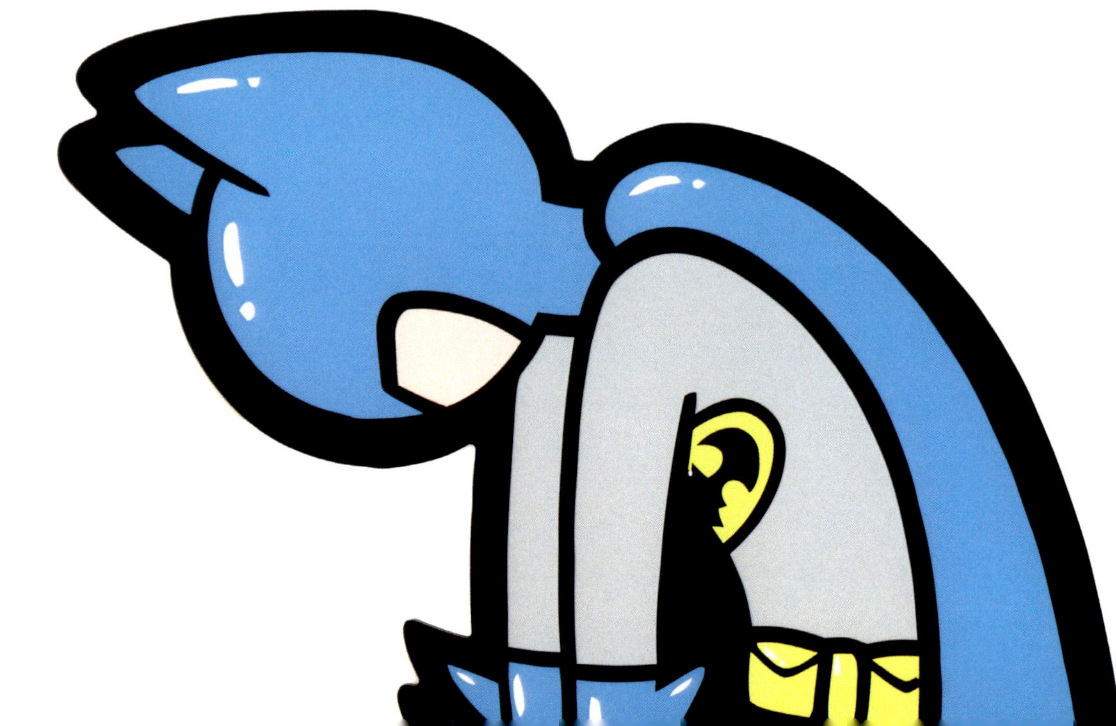

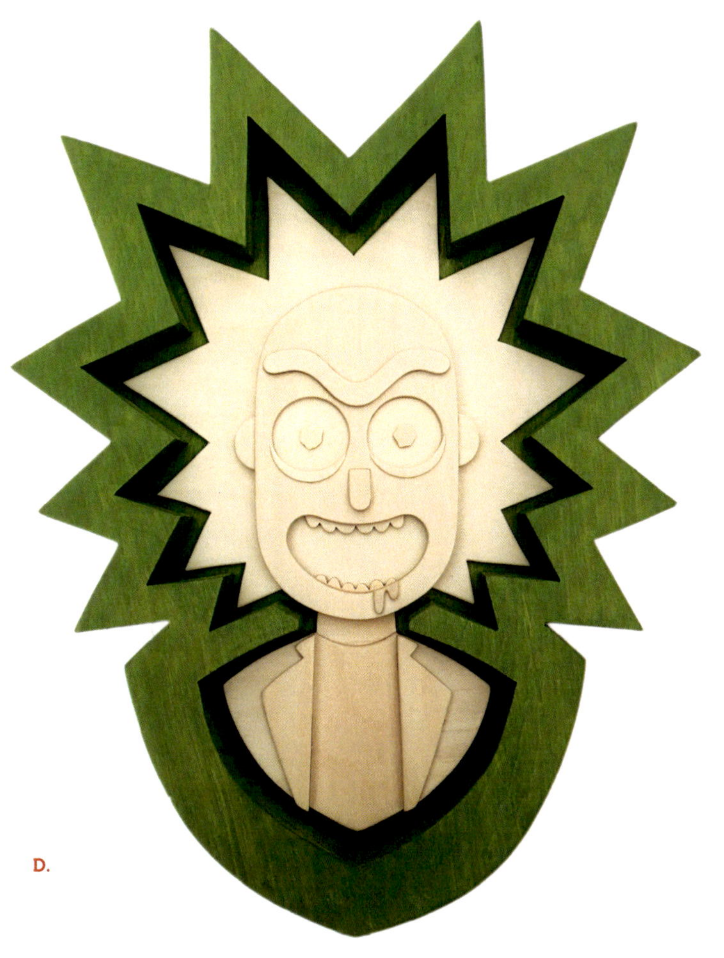

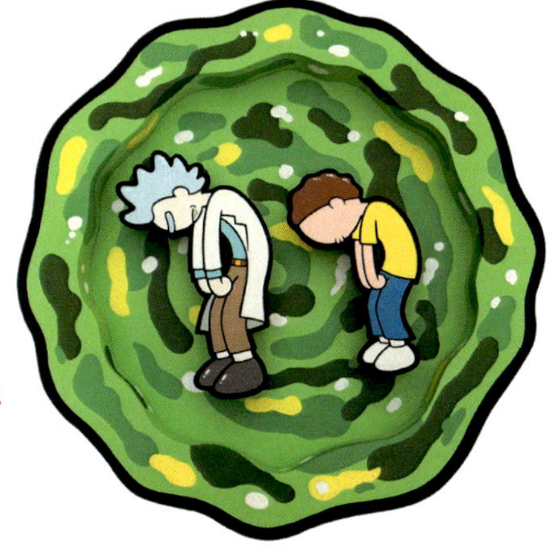

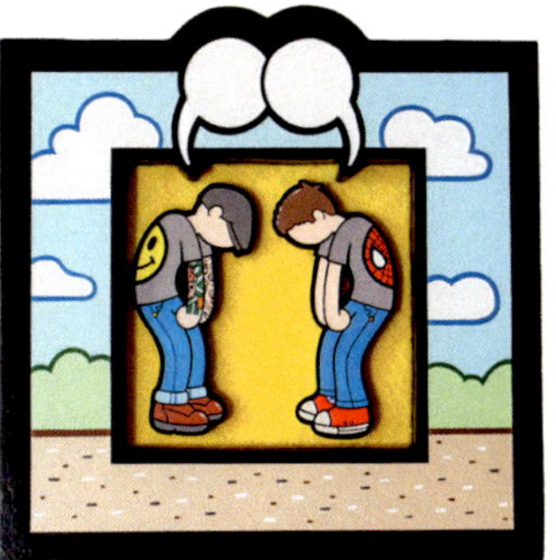

D. *Miles Ritchie*
Rick
wood
10˝ x 12½˝ (2017)

E. *Matt Ritchie*
Ricky & Mort
wood, acrylic paint, plexiglass, felt
13˝ diameter (2017)

F. *Matt Ritchie*
Me & Miles
wood, acrylic paint, plexiglass, felt
8¾˝ x 5½˝ (2017)

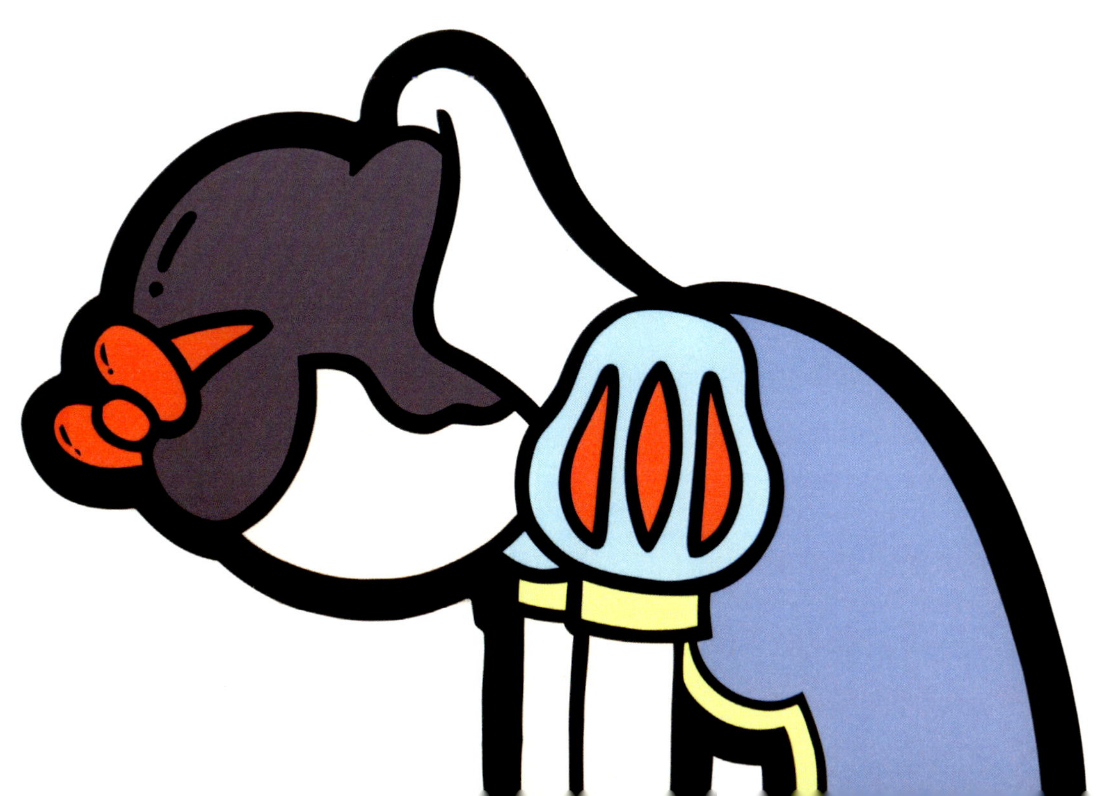

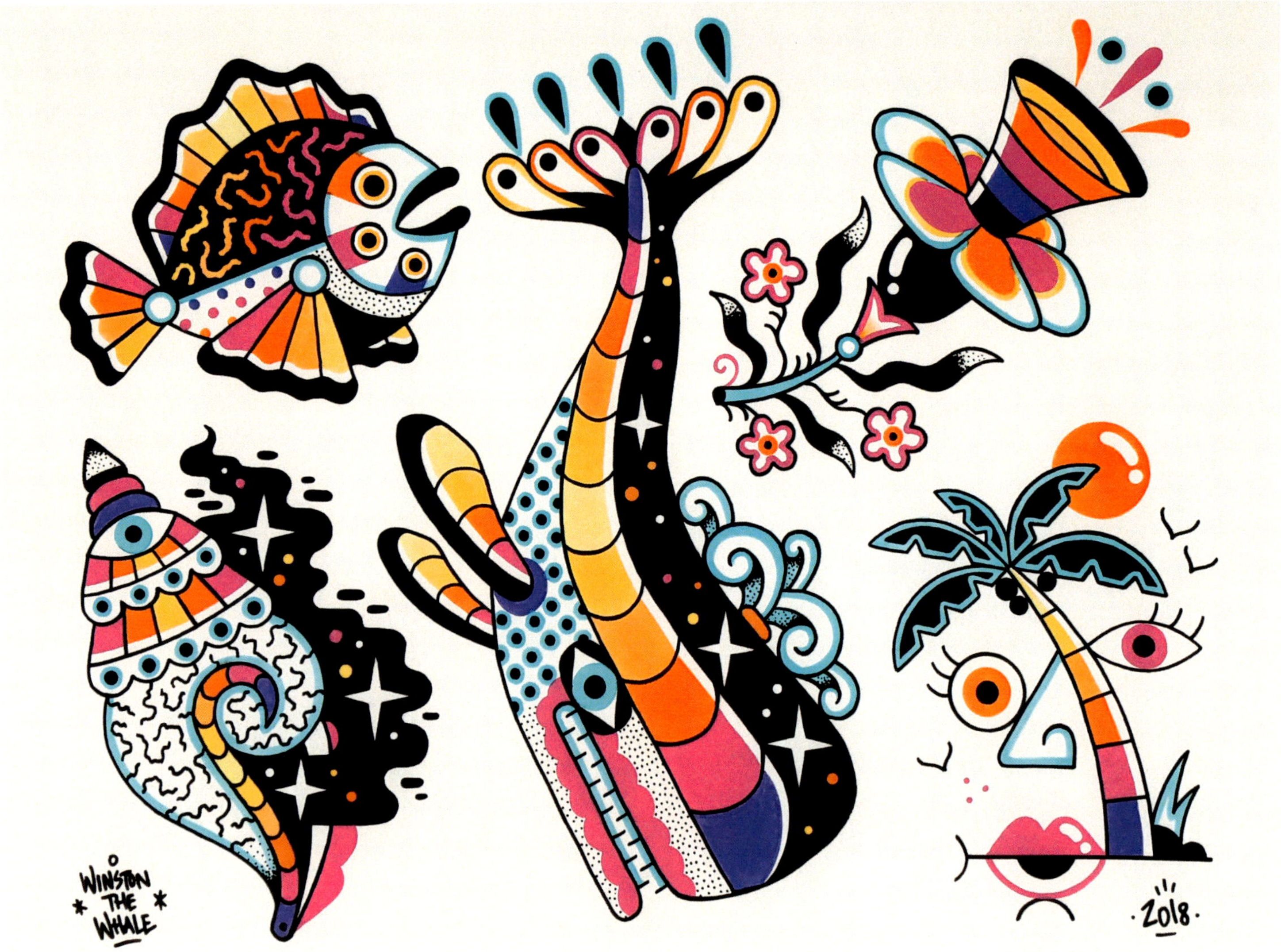

A.

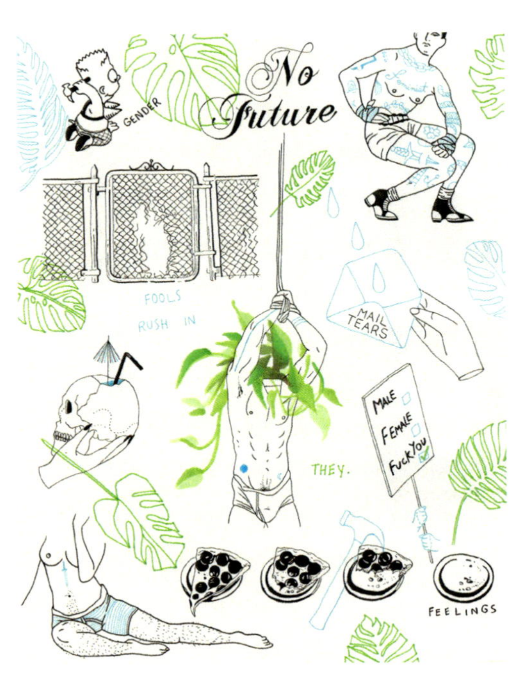

B.

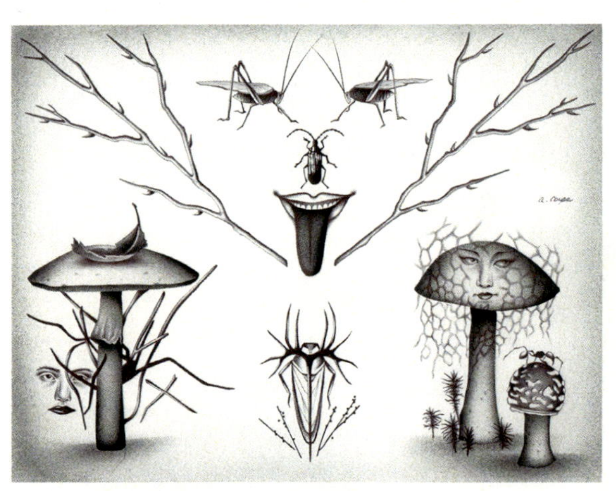

C.

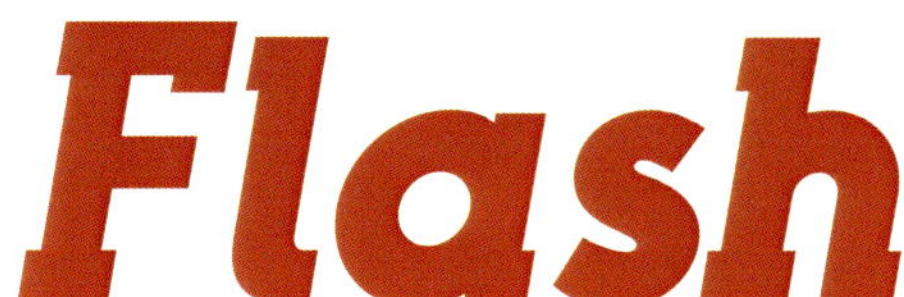

Flash

A Group Exhibition
curated by Dasha Matsuura

February 3—24
2018

Spoke Art SF is pleased to present *FLASH*, a group exhibition featuring over 30 tattoo artists from around the world bringing their own unique style to the ubiquitous tattoo flash sheet. Building on the rich visual history of tattooing, FLASH brings the contemporary parlor into the gallery.

Working in a wide variety of styles, each work has been created by an actively tattooing artist. Freed from the bounds of the increasing demand for custom and client-driven work, each flash sheet represents the artists' personal art practice.

Participating Artists:

Albie • Carlo Amen • Jeremy Ross Armstrong • Holi Barahati • Charline Bataille • Louis Bicycle • Stephanie Brown • Joseph Cassina • Jess Chen • Nomi Chi • Tati Compton • Arielle Coupe • Mike Davis • Henry Hablak • Rachel Hauer • Sera Helen • Jeery Ilkenhon • Ross K Jones • Caleb Kilby • Jess Koala • Rex LC • Matt Leibowitz • Henry Lewis • Noel'le Longhaul • MAB • Andrew Mann • Talia Migliaccio • Curt Montgomery • Lauren Napalitano • Niña Piña • Duke Riley • rat666tatt • Sad Amish Tattooer • Suzani • Meg Tuey • Amanda Wachob • Jan Willem • Winston the Whale • Laura Yahna • Jessica Zed

A. *Winston the Whale*
Tropical Vibes
archival pigment print
edition of 50
14" x 11" (2018)

B. *Lee D'angelo*
No Future
ink on paper
11" x 14" (2018)

C. *Arielle Coupe*
The Ancient Stalker
ink & ballpoint pen on paper
11" x 14" (2018)

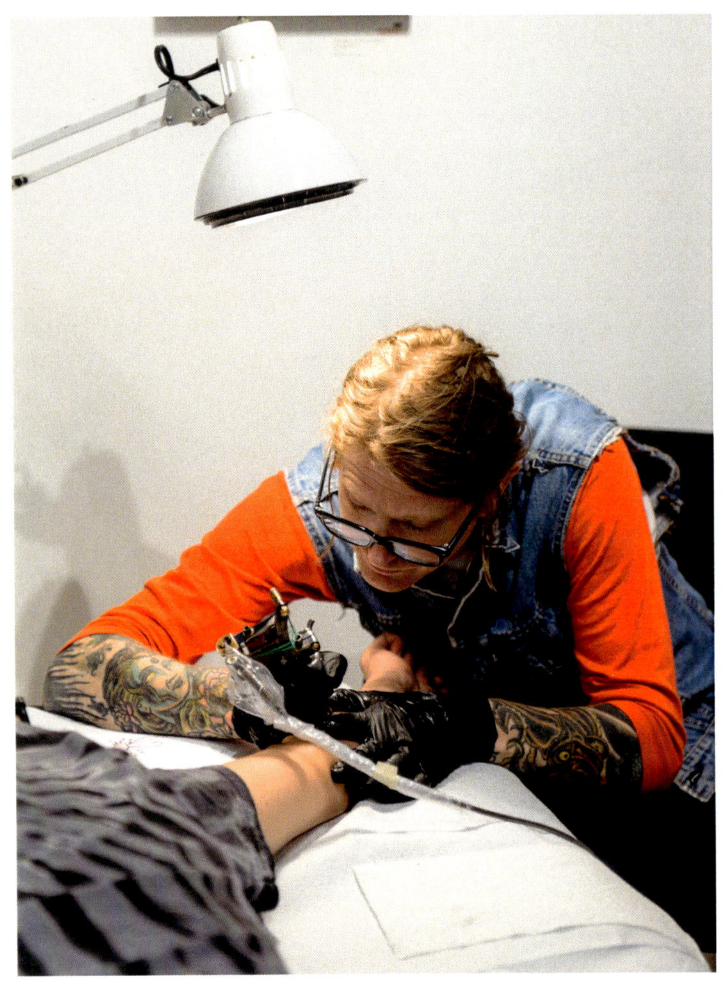

A.

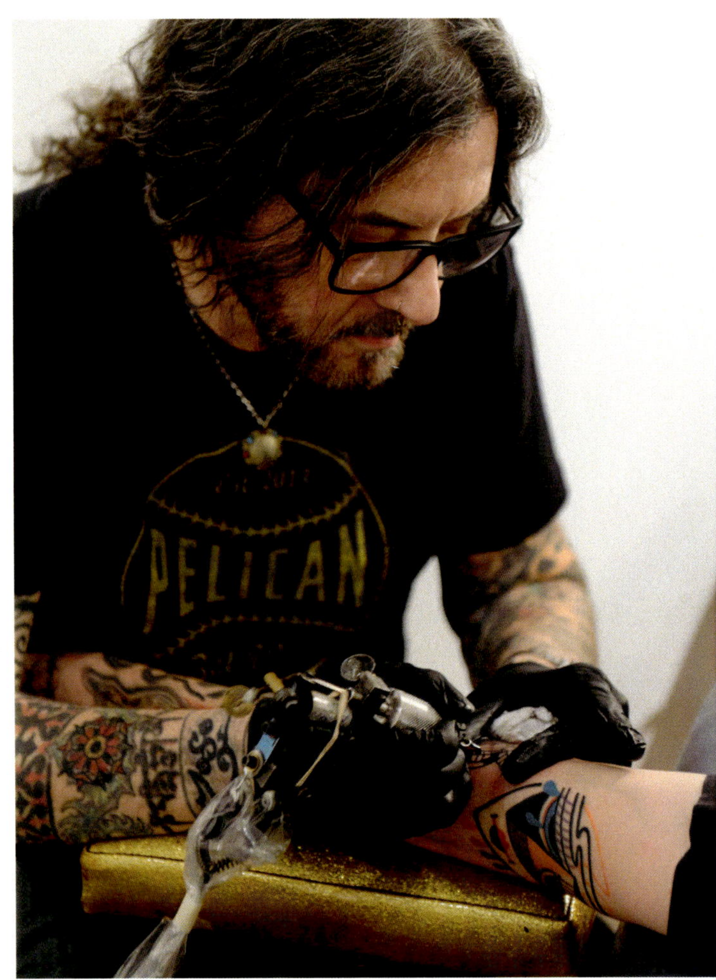

B.

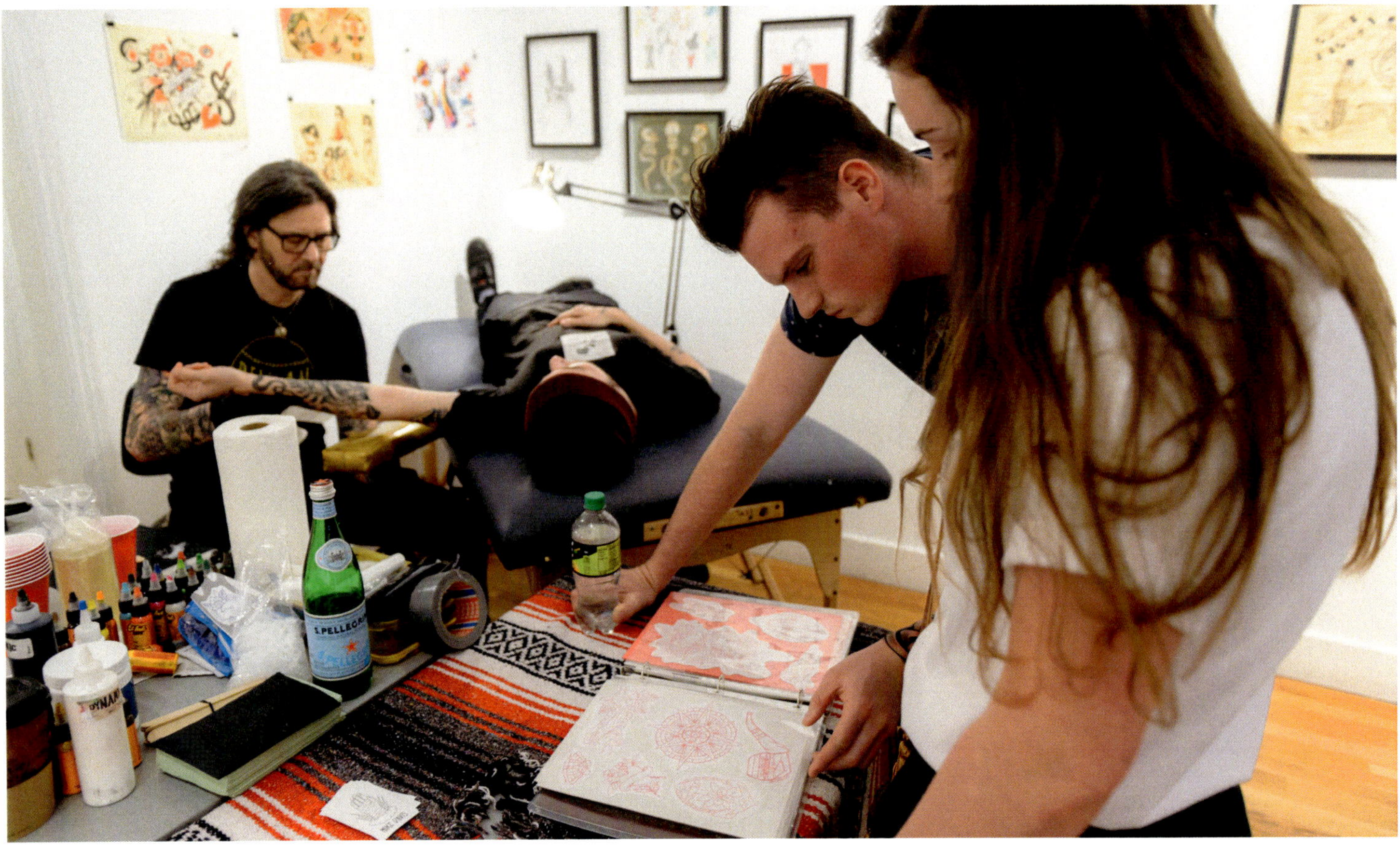

C.

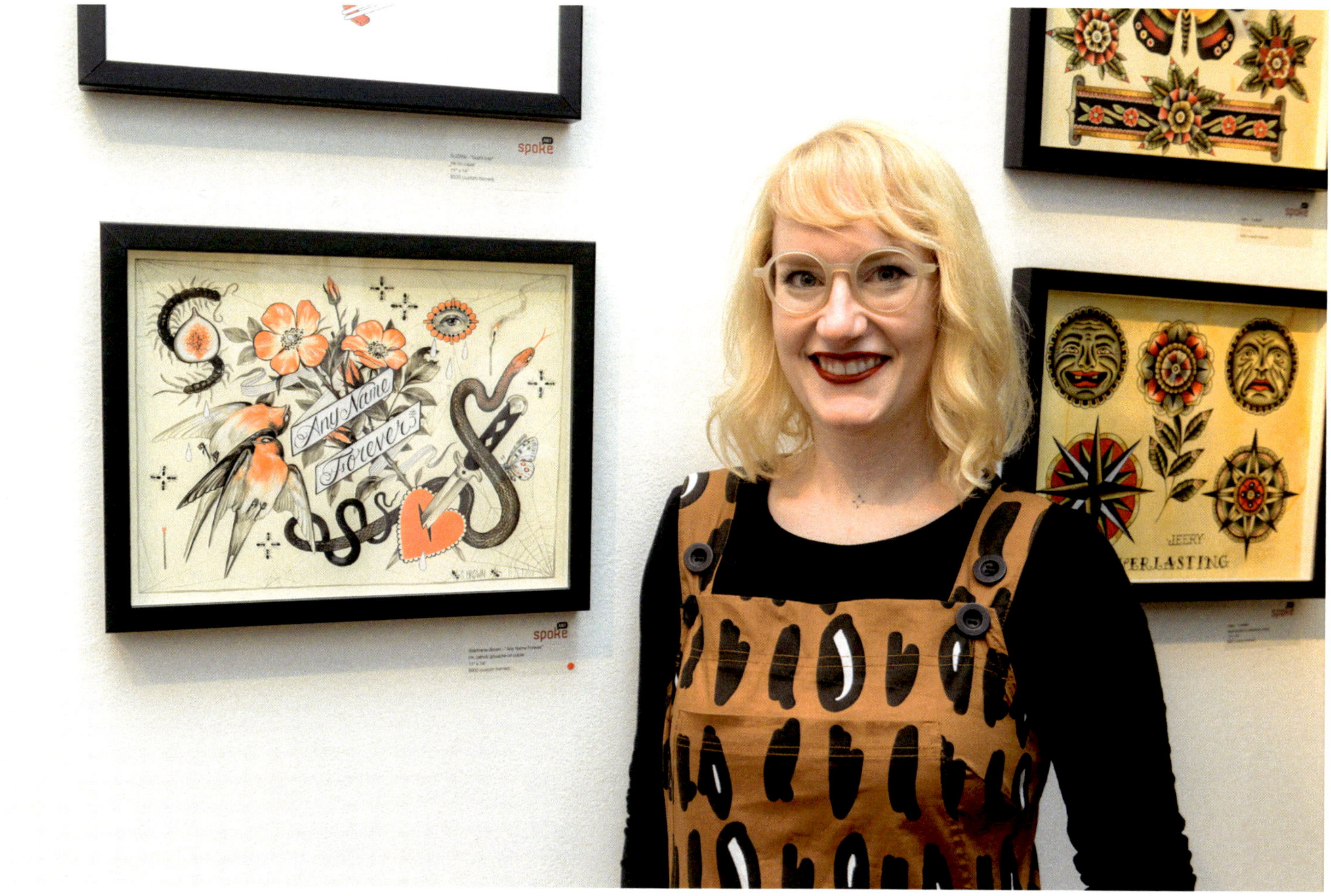

D.

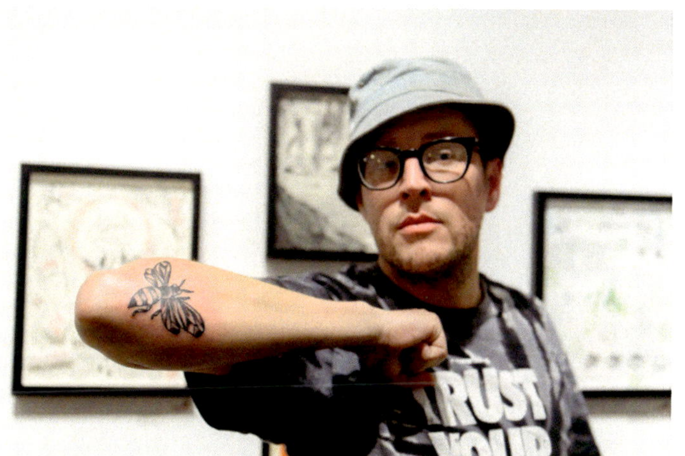

E.

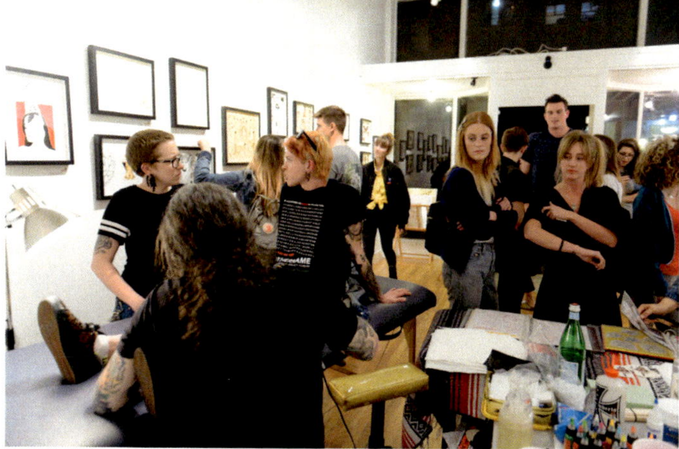

A.
Jeery

B.
Mike Davis

C.
Visitors browsing Mike Davis'
Flash Tattoo Binder

D.
Stephanie Brown

E. & F.
Opening Reception

PHOTOS: Shaun Roberts

F.

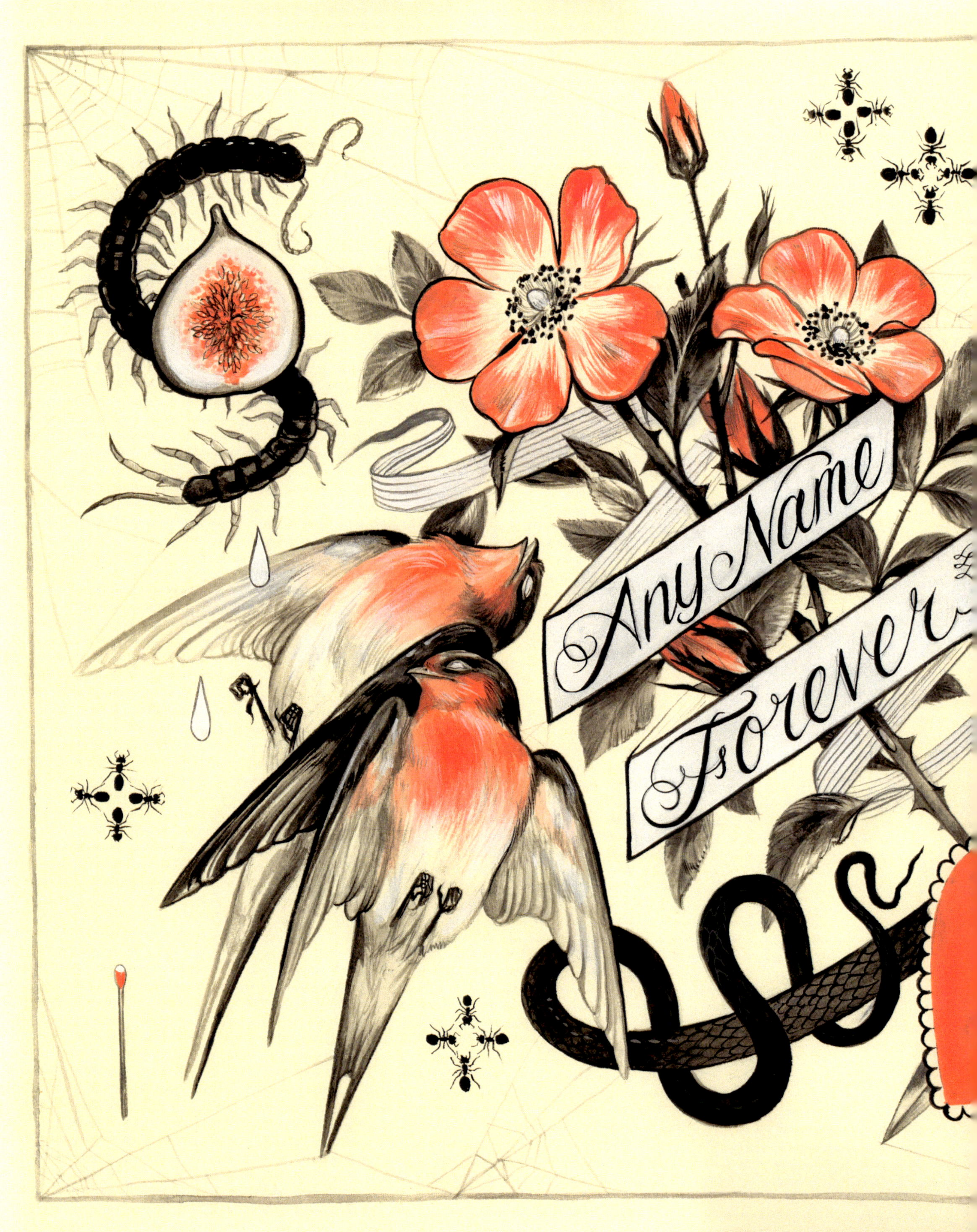

A.

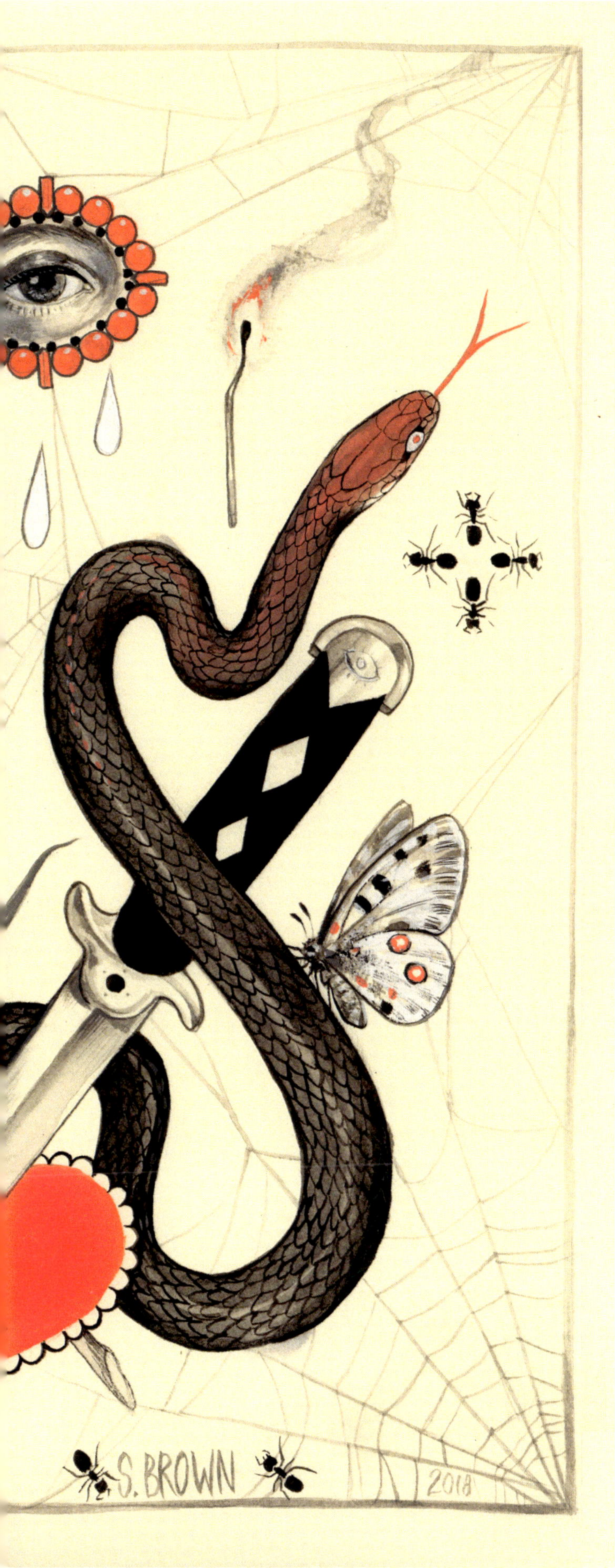

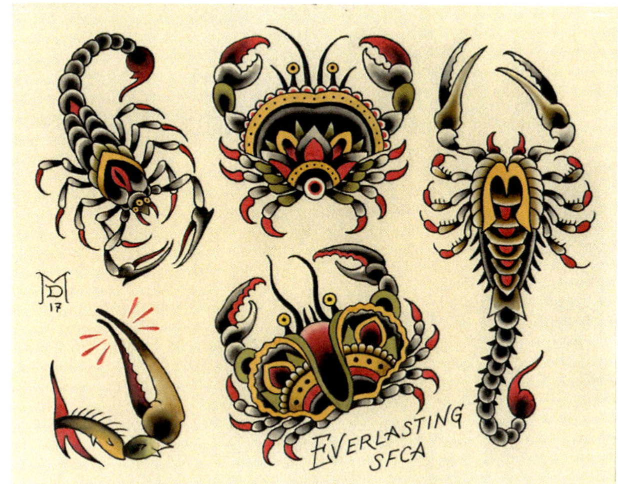

B.

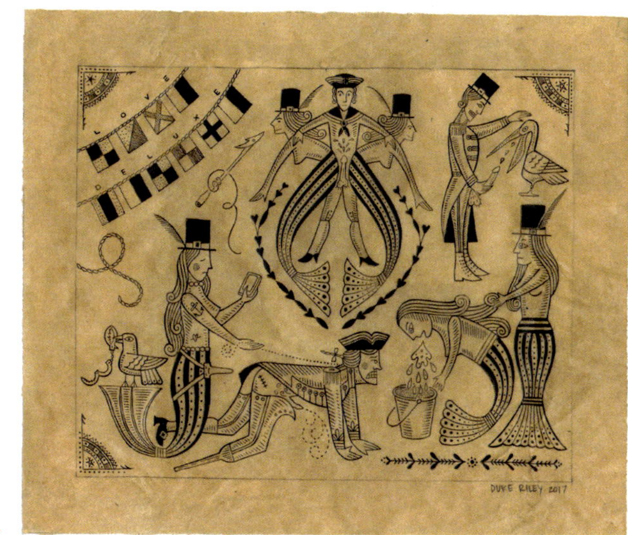

C.

A. **Stephanie Brown**

Any Name Forever

ink, pencil, gouache on paper
14" x 11" (2018)

B. **Mike Davis**

Flash (Crabs)

watercolor on paper
11" x 14" (2017)

C. **Duke Riley**

Love Deluxe

ink on canary paper
11" x 14" (2017)

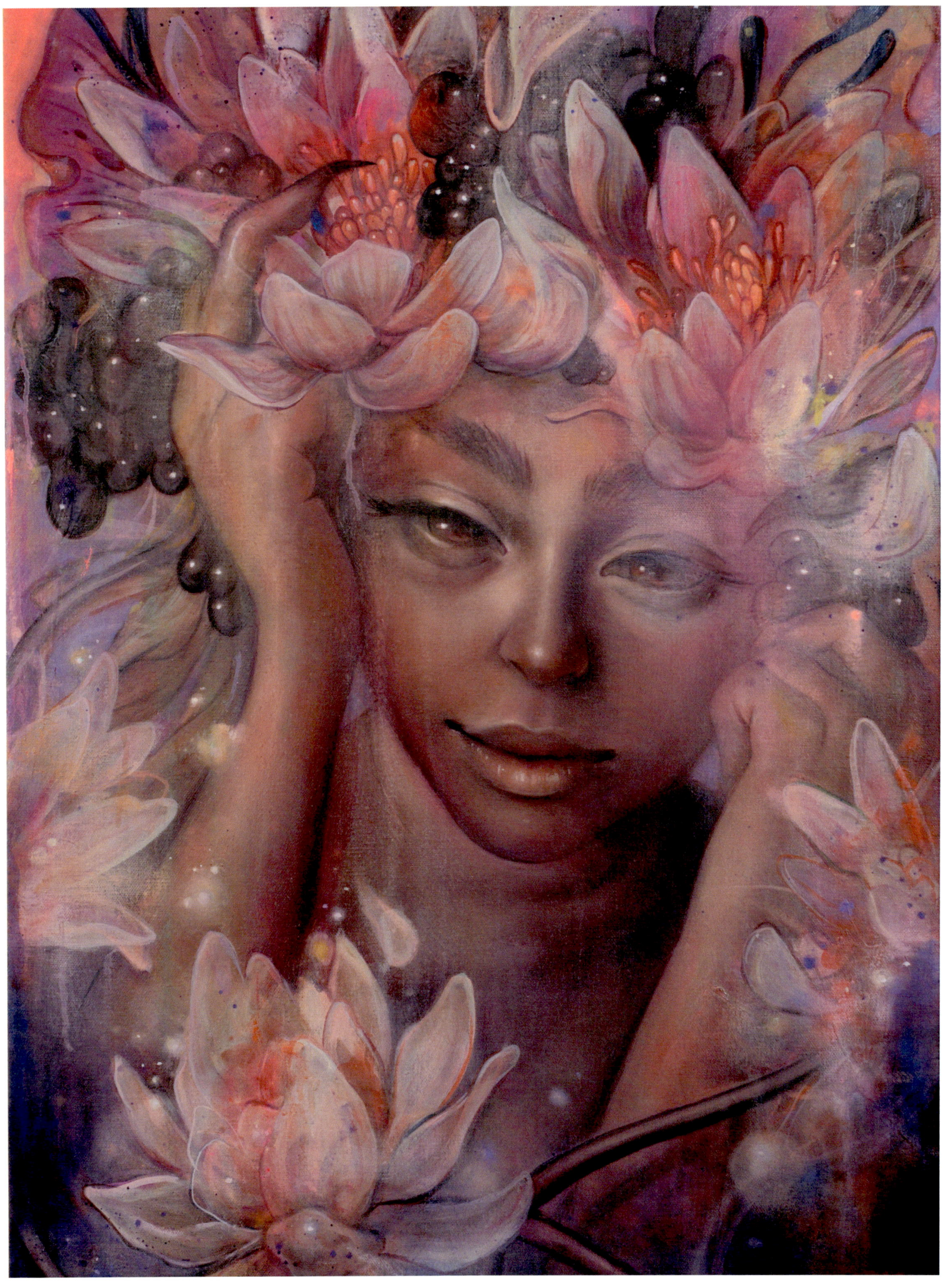

Nymphaea

Tatiana Suarez

March 3—24
2018

Spoke SF is pleased to present *Nymphaea*, a solo exhibition by Miami-based painter Tatiana Suarez. For her inaugural solo exhibition at Spoke Art, Suarez has created an ethereal body of paintings and watercolors continuing to explore the tropical world she has constructed for her darkly-sensual feminine figures.

Inspired by the folklore and mythology of her hometown and heritage, Suarez has created a world rich with symbolism and history. The lotus flowers and lilies, much like the women within the work exude a sense of strength and rebirth, emerging from the murky, uncertain waters.

Tatiana Suarez
Marã
oil on canvas
20" x 30" (2018)

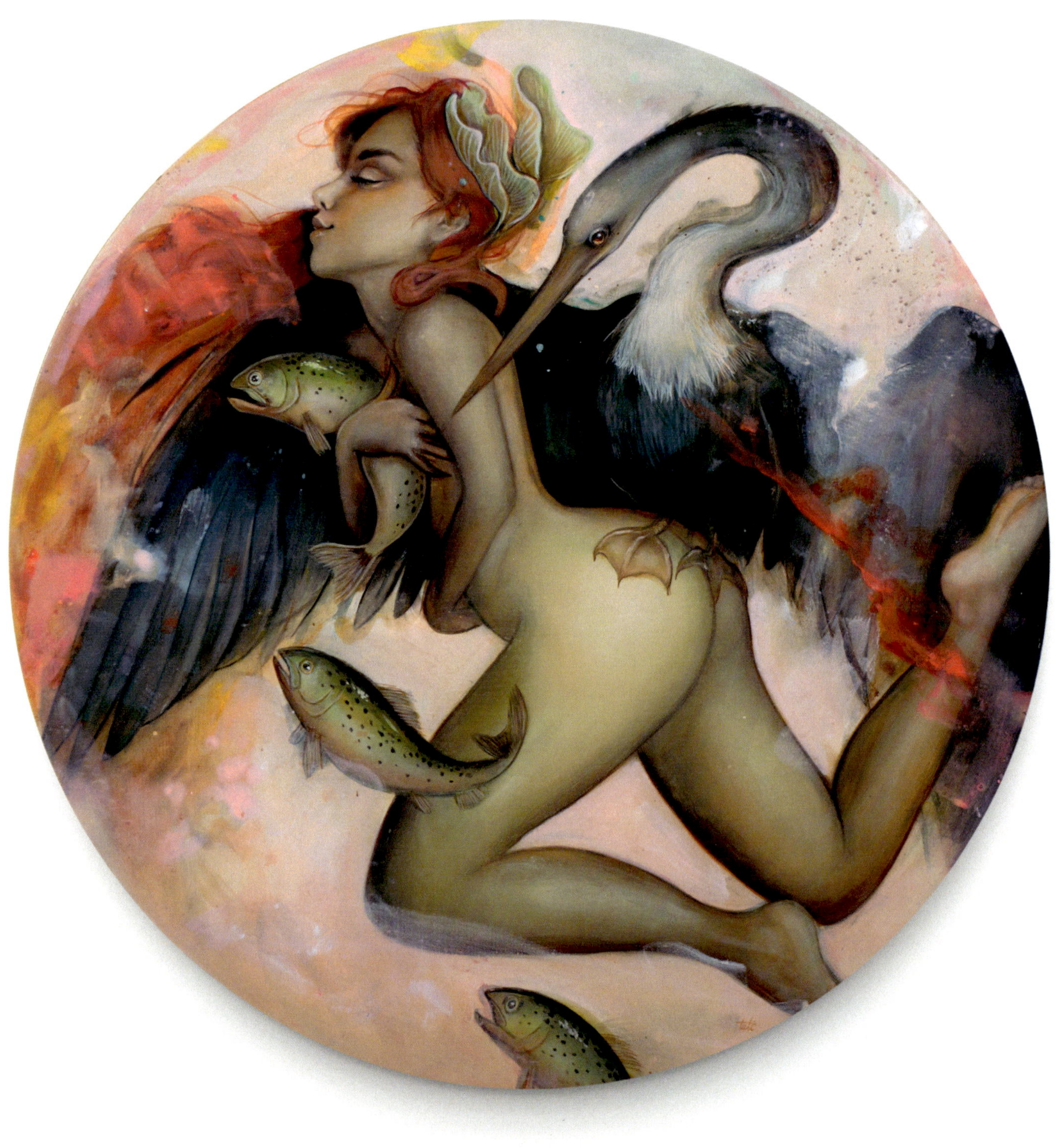

Tatiana Suarez

*Everything is
Coming Together*

oil on canvas

22″ diameter (2018)

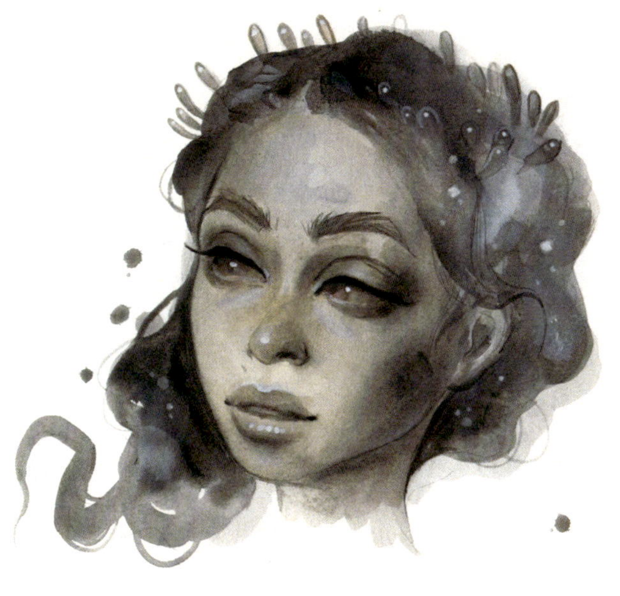

A.

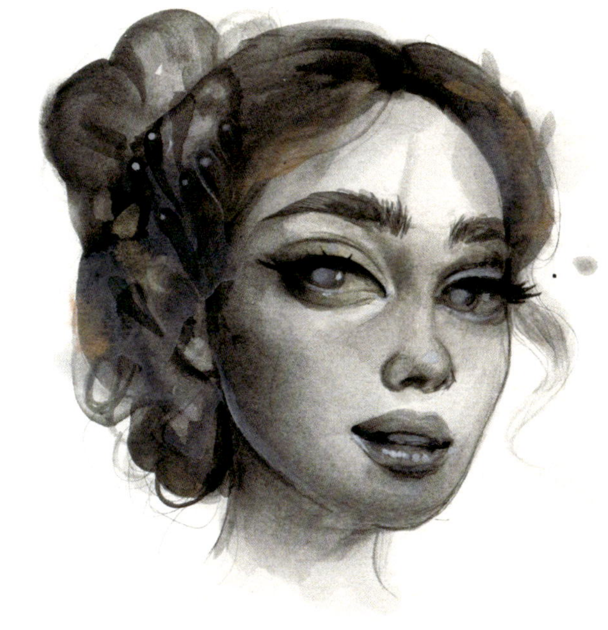

B.

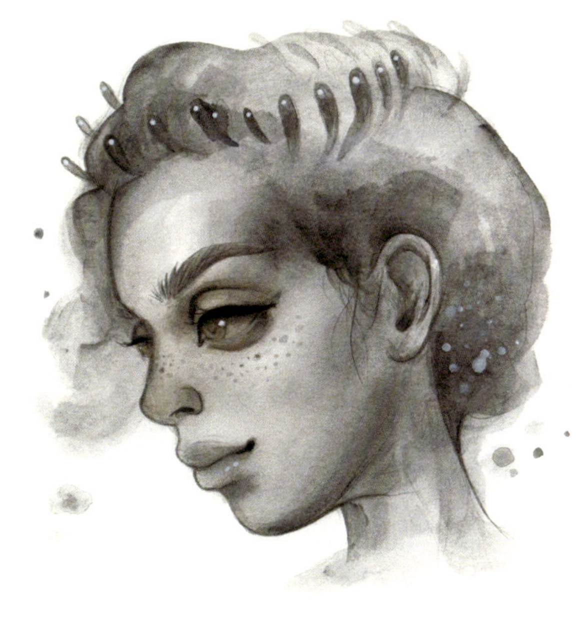

C.

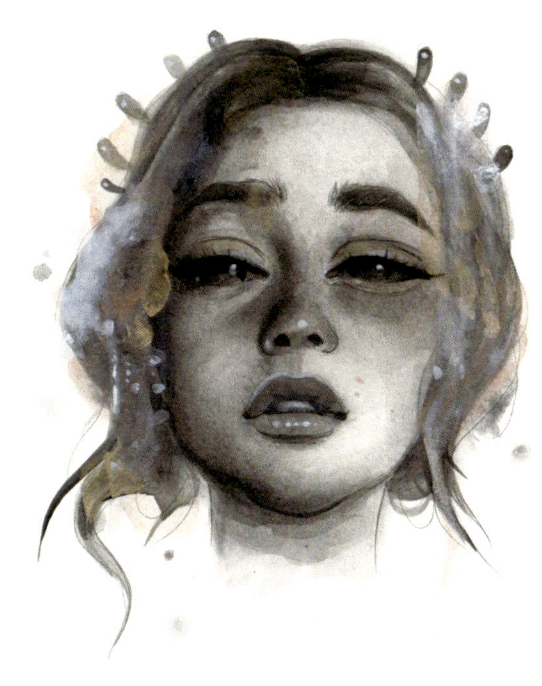

D.

A. **Tatiana Suarez**
Ana
watercolor on paper
8˝ x 8˝ (2018)

B. **Tatiana Suarez**
Ceci
watercolor on paper
8˝ x 8˝ (2018)

C. **Tatiana Suarez**
Laila
watercolor on paper
8˝ x 8˝ (2018)

D. **Tatiana Suarez**
Leslie
watercolor on paper
8˝ x 8˝ (2018)

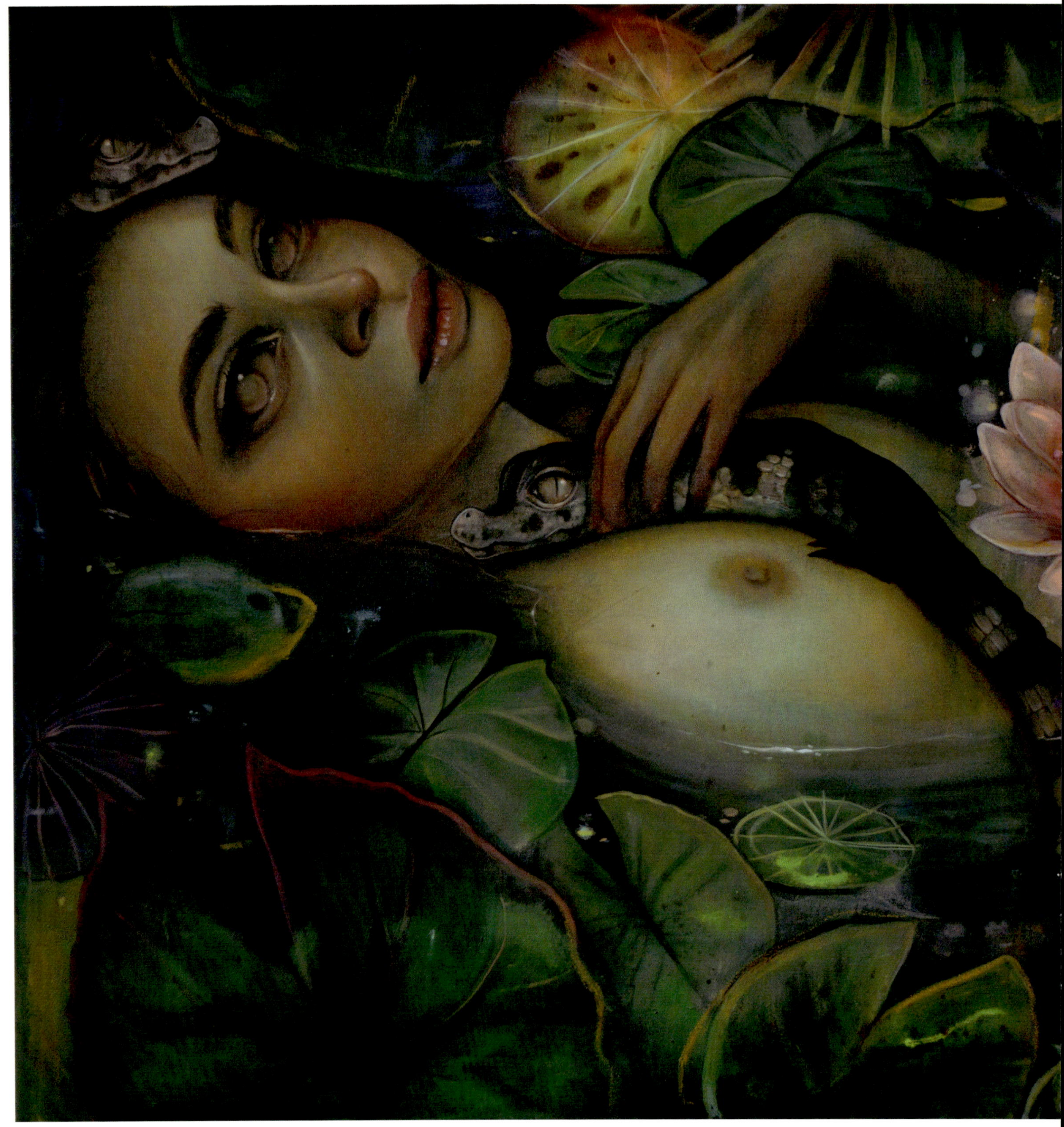

Lúna

oil on canvas
36˝ x 48˝ (2018)

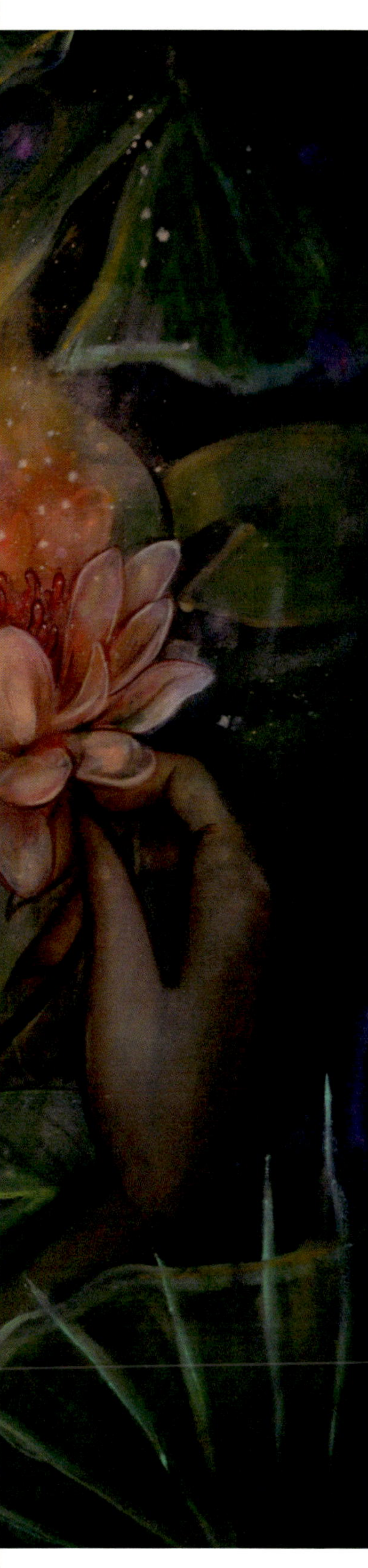

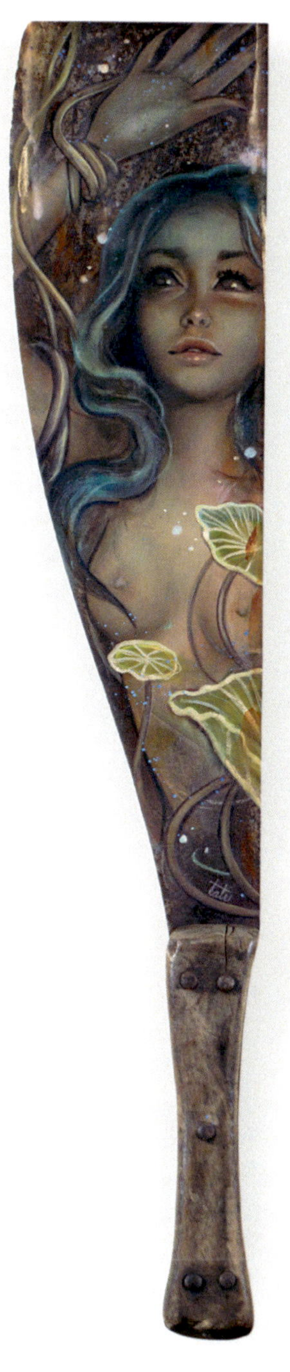

Tatiana Suarez

Entangled

oil on machete
3¼˝ x 21½˝ (2018)

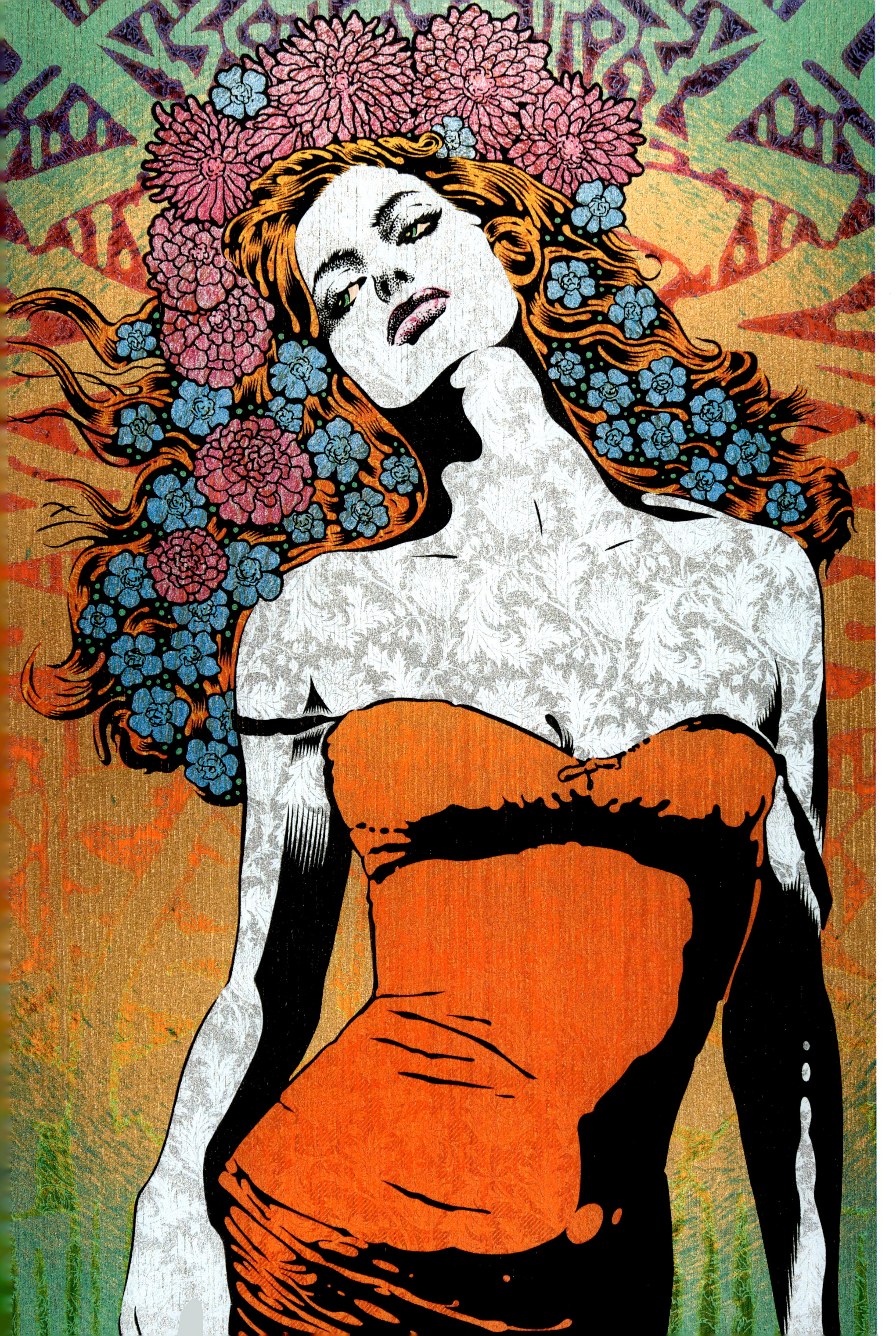

Heaven of Many a Tangled Hue

Chuck Sperry

April 7–28
2018

Spoke SF is pleased to present *Heaven of Many a Tangled Hue*, a solo exhibition by the prolific San Francisco-based artist and master screen printer *Chuck Sperry*. For his third solo exhibition with Spoke Art, Sperry has created a verdant garden of new work tended by his signature shimmering muses.

Informed by art historical figures such as Gustave Moreau and William Morris, combined with the poetry of P.B. Shelley, Greek Mythology and his home in the Haight-Ashbury neighborhood of San Francisco, Chuck Sperry has cultivated a distinct style brimming with exuberance and energy. Combined with his masterful printing expertise, Sperry creates ethereal and psychedelically saturated screen prints that draw crowds and dedicated fans around the world.

Chuck Sperry
Erato
7 color screen print on oak panel
edition of 30
20˝ x 30˝ (2018)

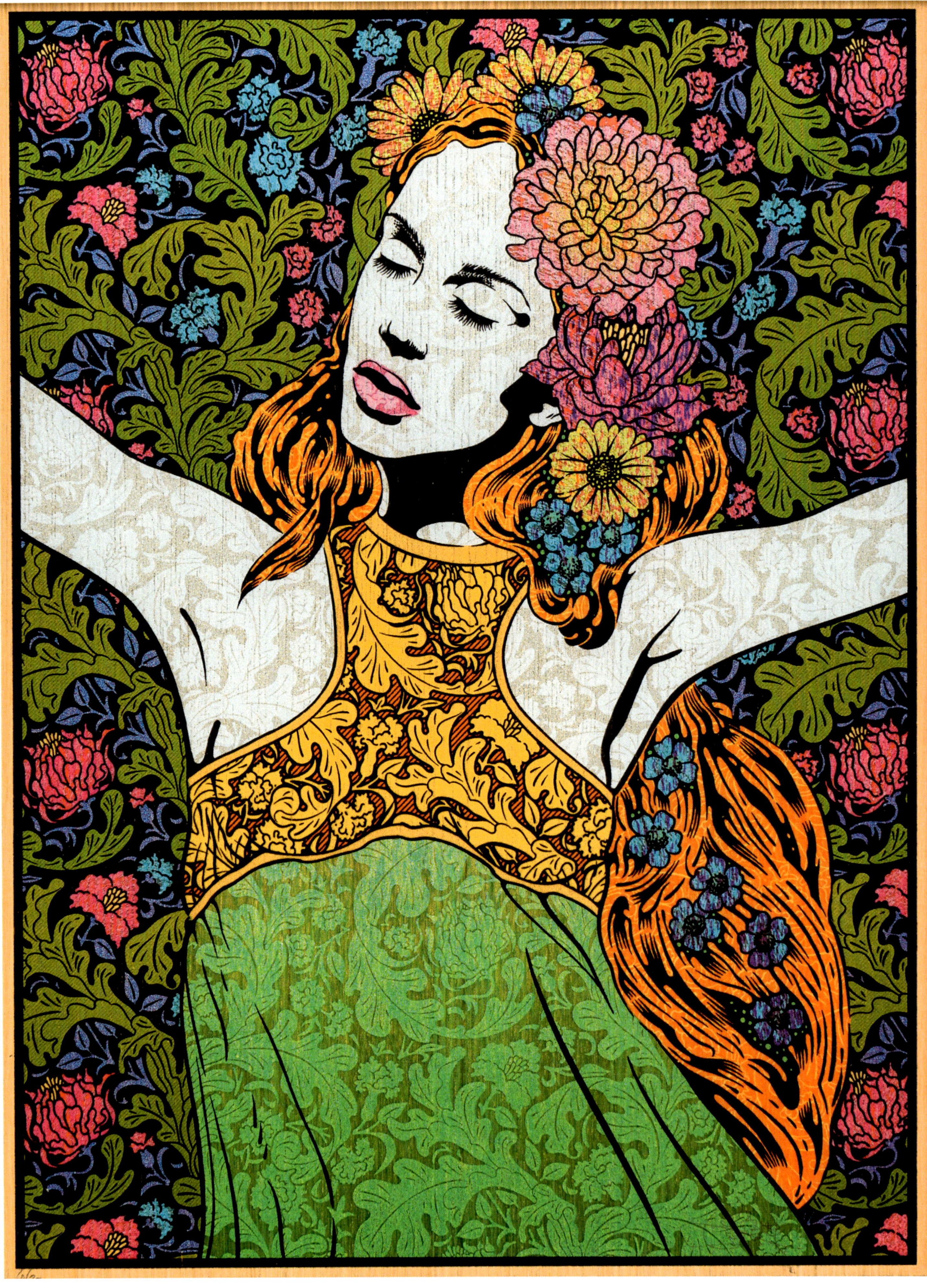

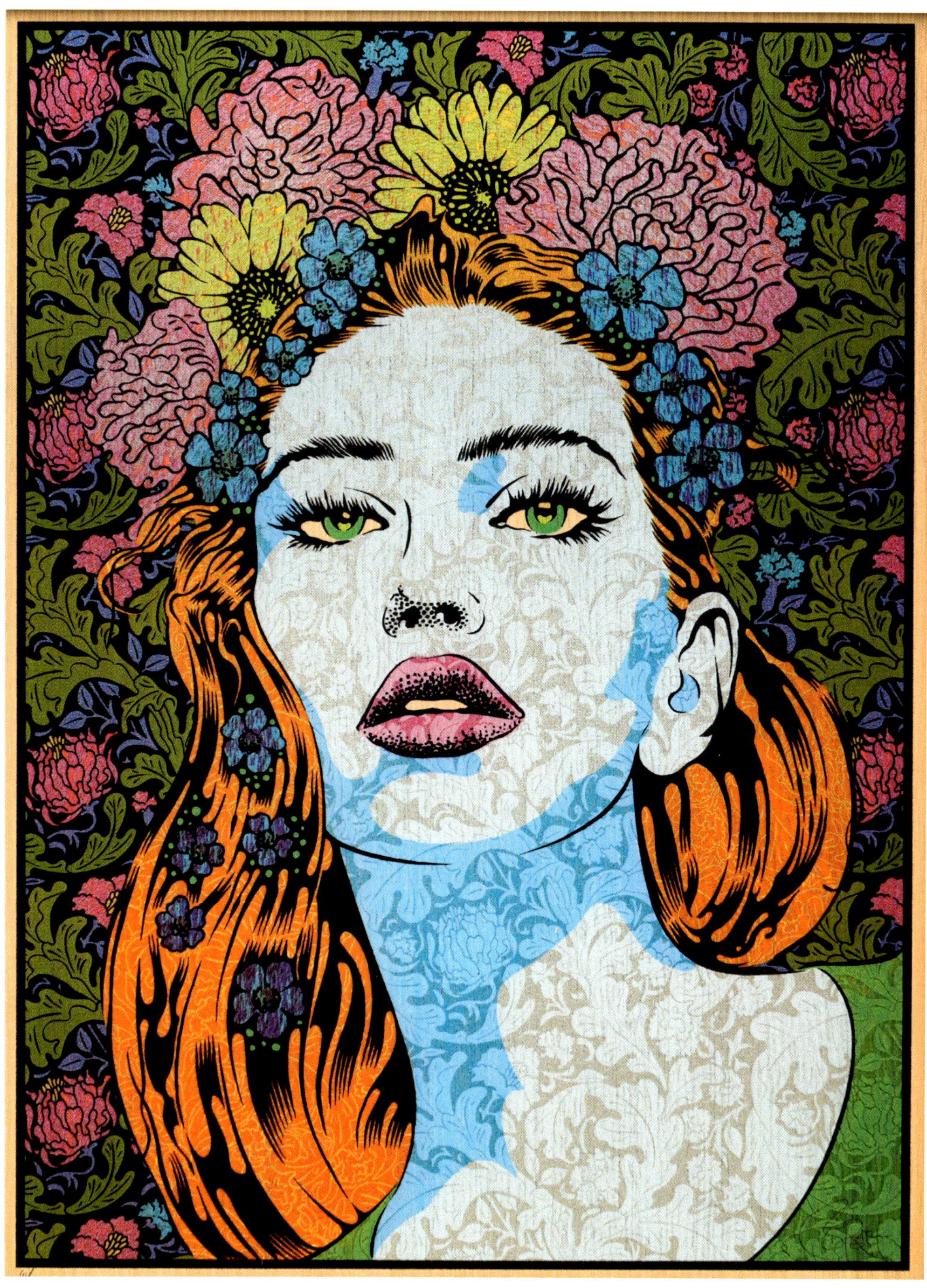

Chuck Sperry

Rhyme

7 color screen print on oak panel
edition of 30
18" x 24" (2018)

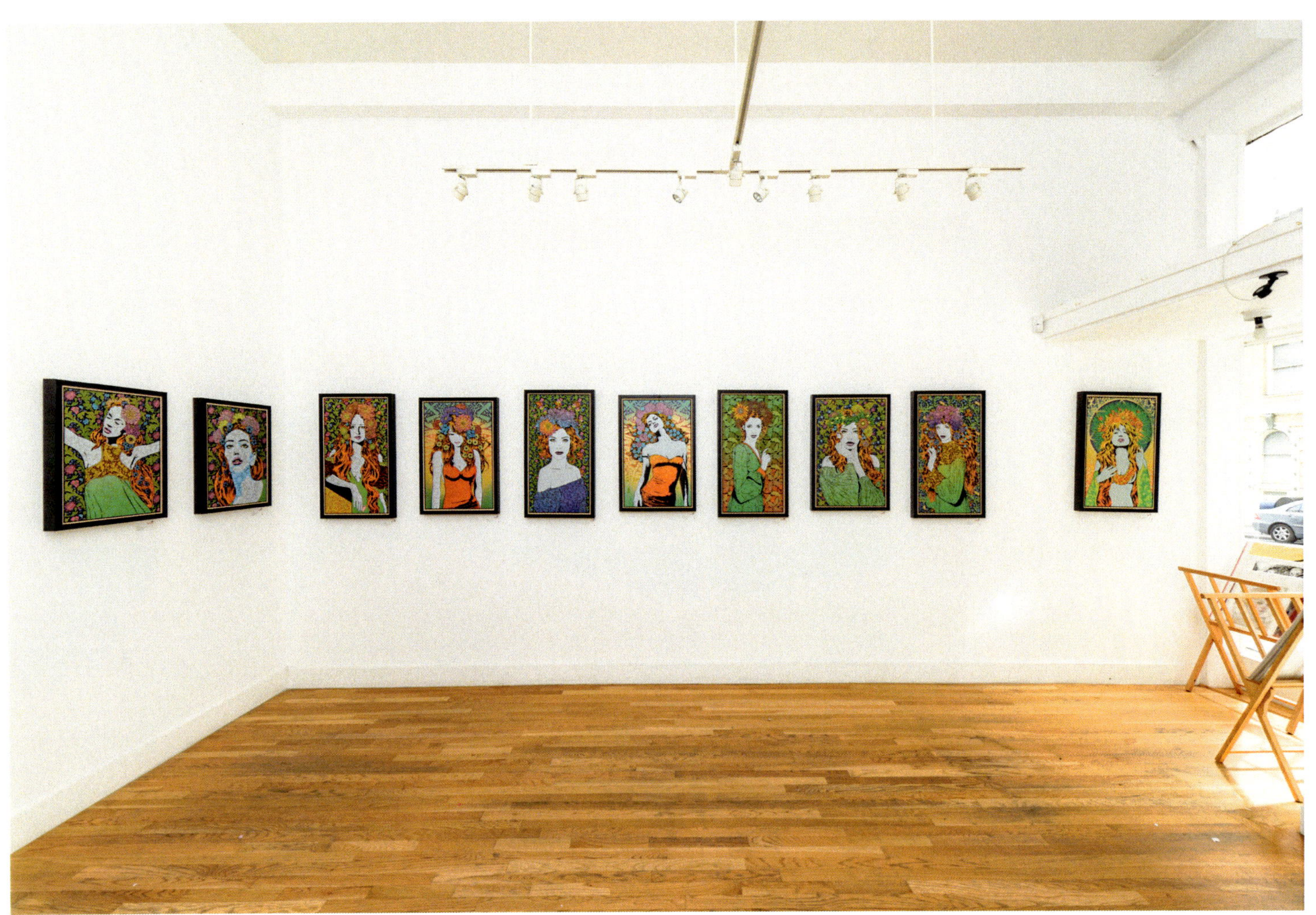

Installation View
PHOTO: Shaun Roberts

Opening Reception
PHOTOS: Shaun Roberts

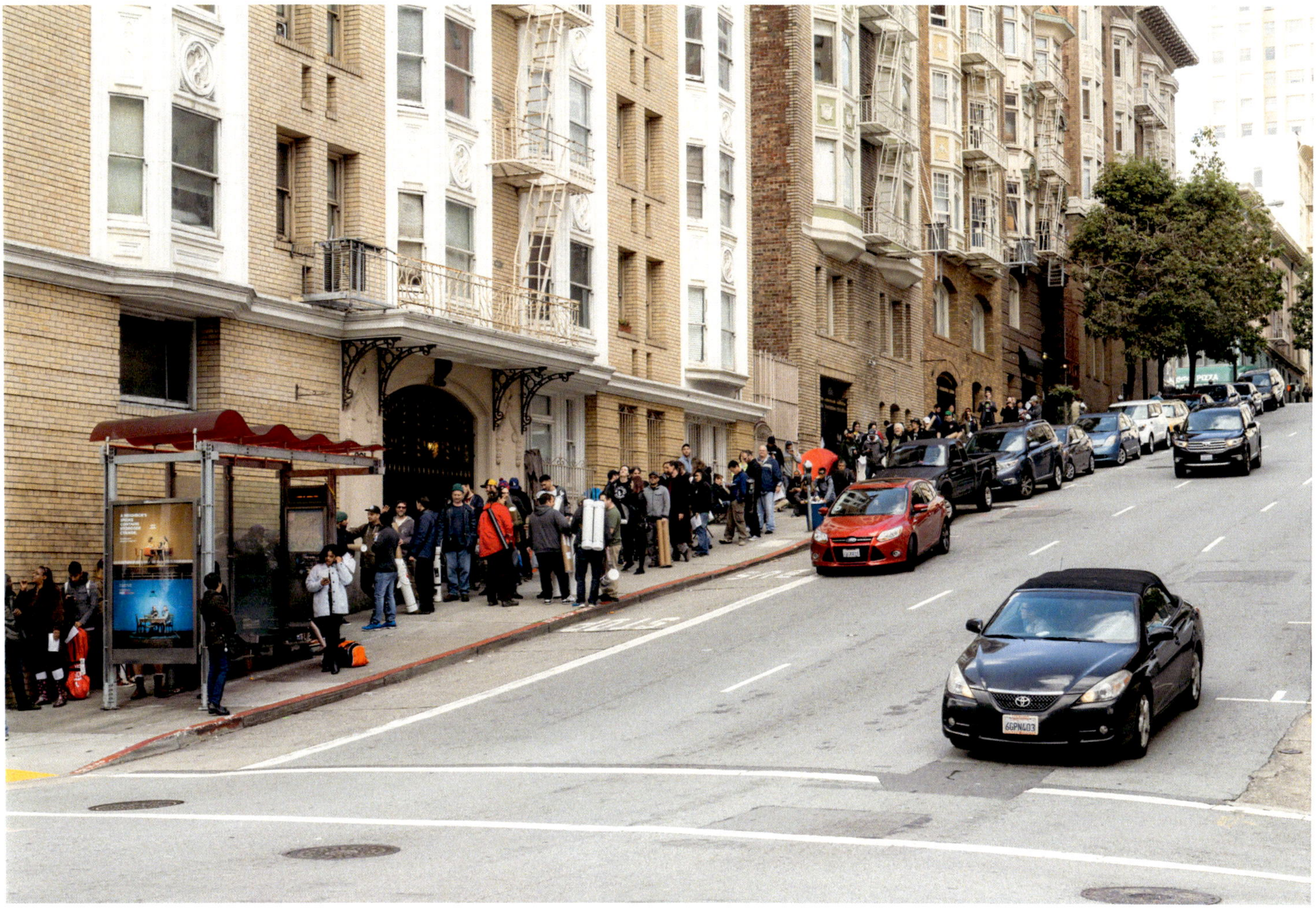

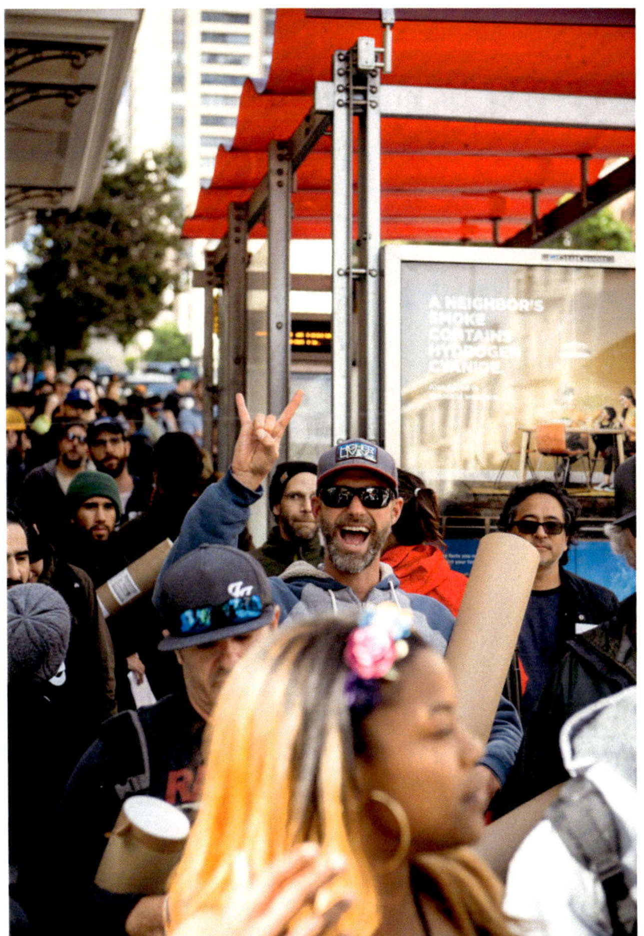

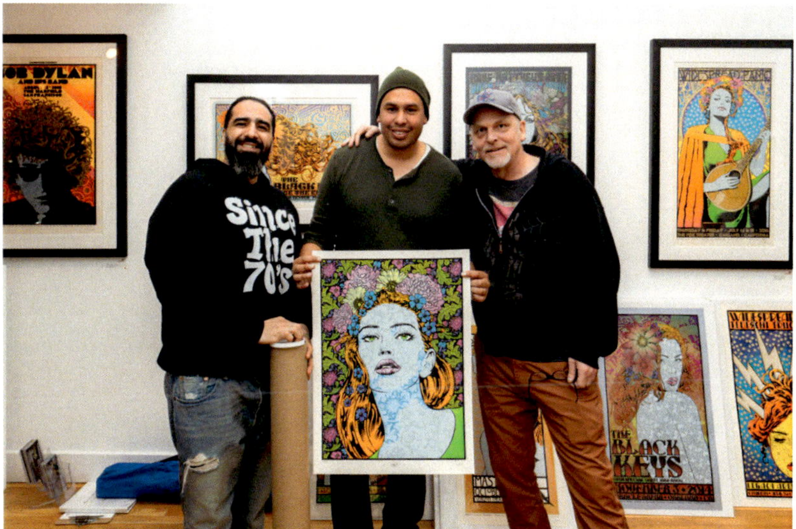

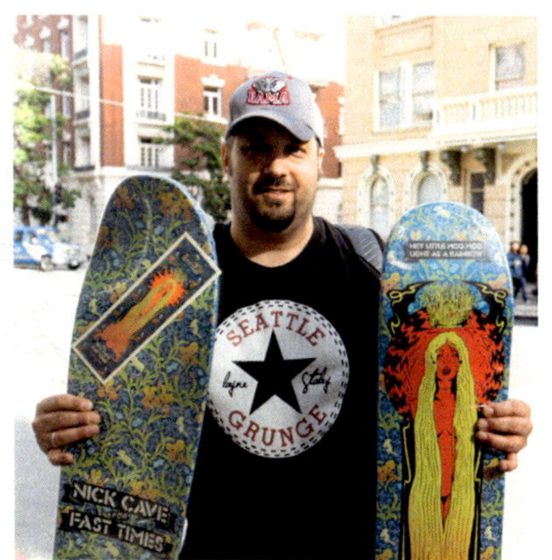
SEATTLE
GRUNGE
NICK CAVE
FAST TIMES

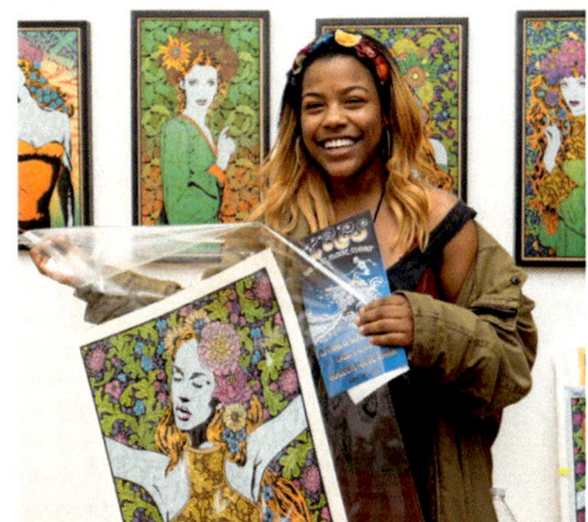

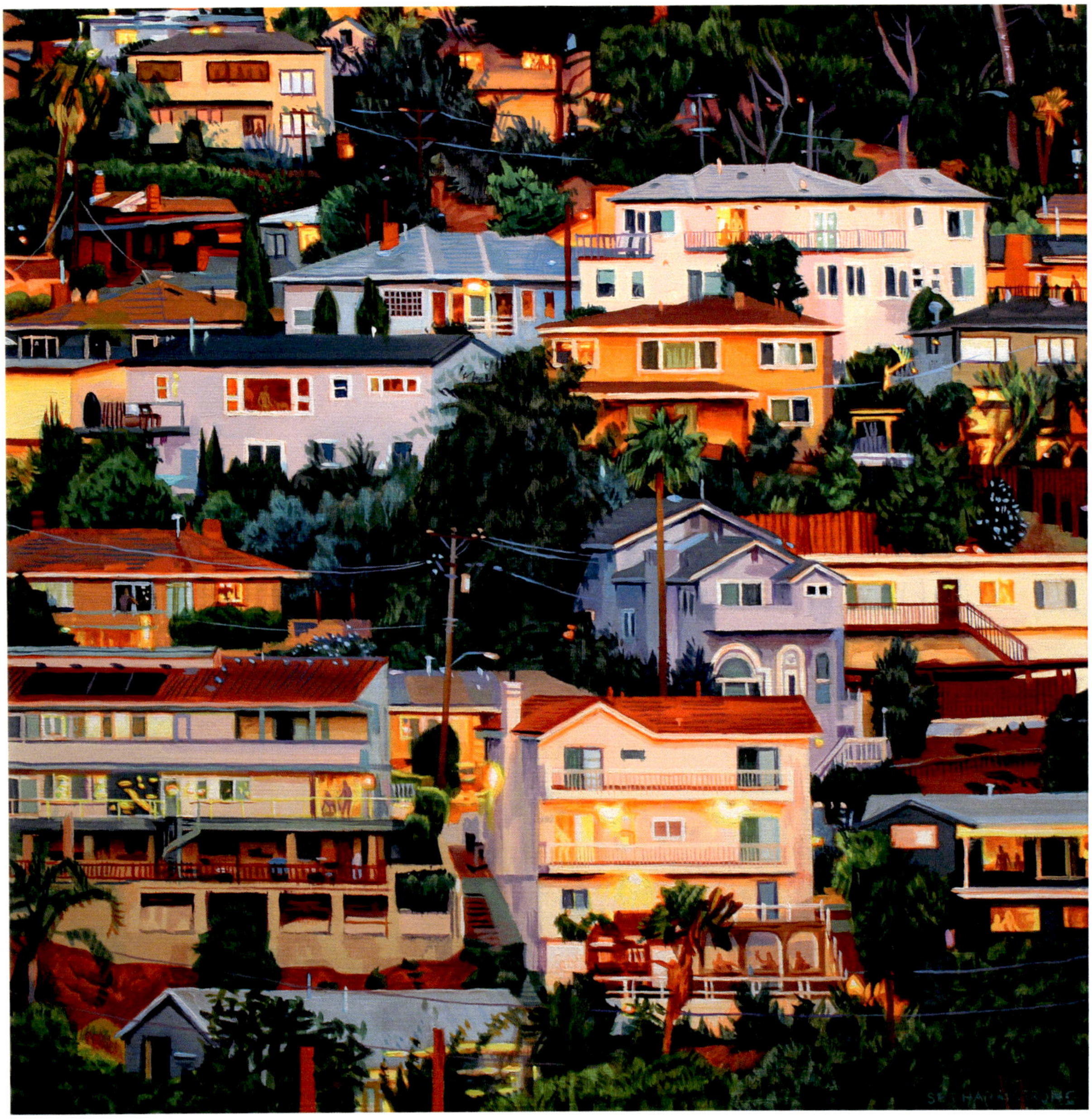

A.

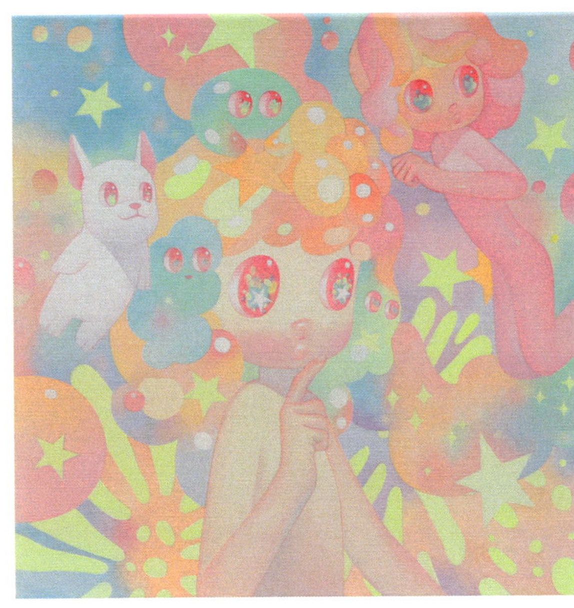

B.

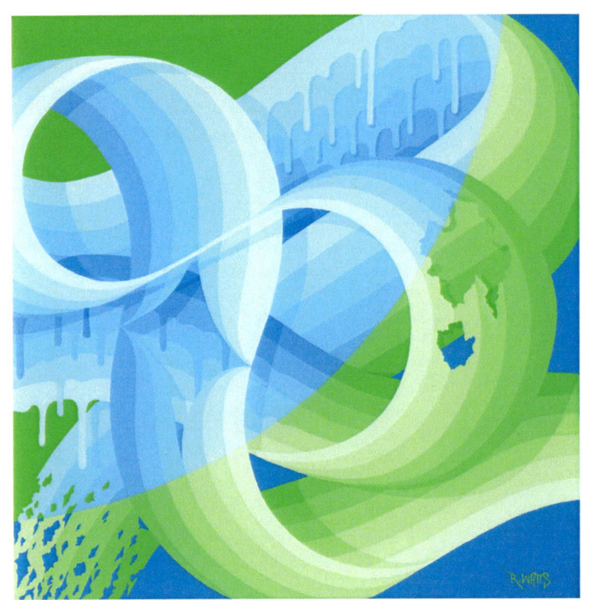

C.

12 x 12

A Group Exhibition

May 5—26
2018

Spoke Art is pleased to present *12 x 12*, a dynamic group exhibition featuring over 50 local and international artists working in a 12 x 12 format. We challenged some of our favorite artists to work within a 12 x 12 inch space and left the rest up to them. The result is a stunning display of the endless possibilities contained within the bounds of the composition.

Working in a variety of media including painting, embroidery, sculpture and beyond, each artist presents their unique style while adhering to the size parameters. Figures, landscapes and abstract forms dwell in each piece, inviting the viewer into the realm contained in each work.

Participating Artists:

Peter Adamyan • Seth Armstrong • Glenn Arthur • Bagger 43 • Raul Barquet • Laura Berger • Jonathan Bergeron • Robert Bowen • Lauren Brevner • Leilani Bustamente • Adam Caldwell • David Choong Lee • Sam Wolfe Connelly • Deangus • Jason Edmiston • Ben Frost • Alex Garant • Ken Garduno • Serge Gay Jr. • Abigail Goldman • Greg Gossel • Lauren Gregg • Caitlin Hackett • Happy D • Jessica Hess • Christine Aria Hostetler • Eliza Ivanova • Aaron Jasinski • Yumiko Kayukawa • Susannah Kelly • Caia Koopman • So Youn Lee • Adam Lister • Sergio Lopez • Amanda Lynn • Sean Mahan • Nimit Malavia • Ryan Malley • Jose Mertz • JP Neang • Jeany Ngo • Nicomi Nix Turner • Gage Opdenbrow • Karla Ortiz • Daryll Peirce • Rich Pellegrino • Neil Perry • Kevin Peterson • Mwanel Pierre-Louis • Ferris Plock • Dan Quintana • Carlos Ramirez • Allison Reimold • Ximena Rendon • Mike Shine • Jessica So Ren Tang • Amliv Sotomayor • Deth P Sun • Miranda Tacchia • Kelly Tunstall • Ricky Watts • Casey Weldon

A. *Seth Armstrong*

Orange

oil on panel
12˝ x 12˝ (2018)

B. *So Youn Lee*

Sprinkle

oil and acrylic on linen
12˝ x 12˝ (2018)

C. *Ricky Watts*

Vernal Equinox

acrylic on canvas
12˝ x 12˝ (2018)

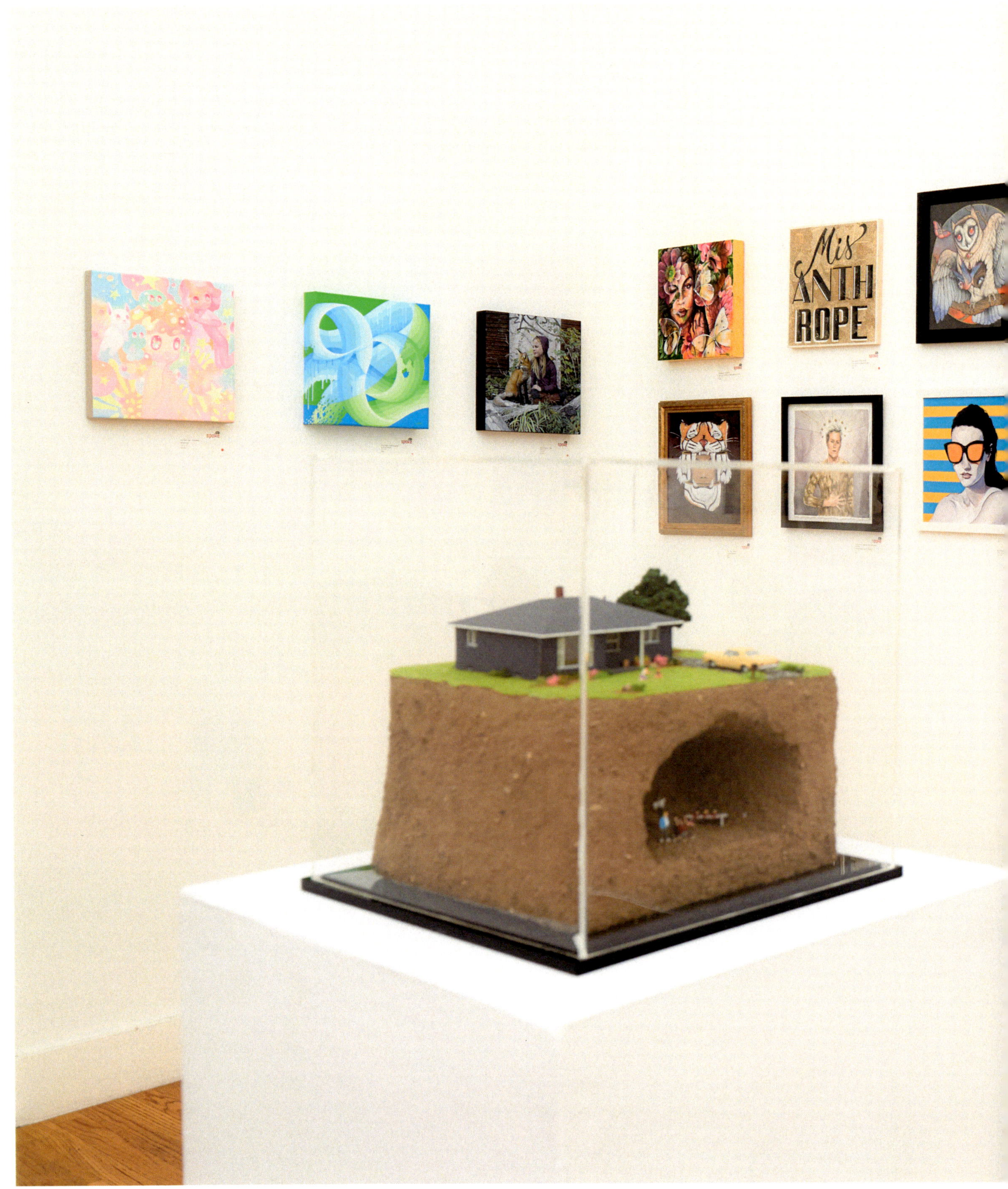

Installation View
PHOTO: Shaun Roberts

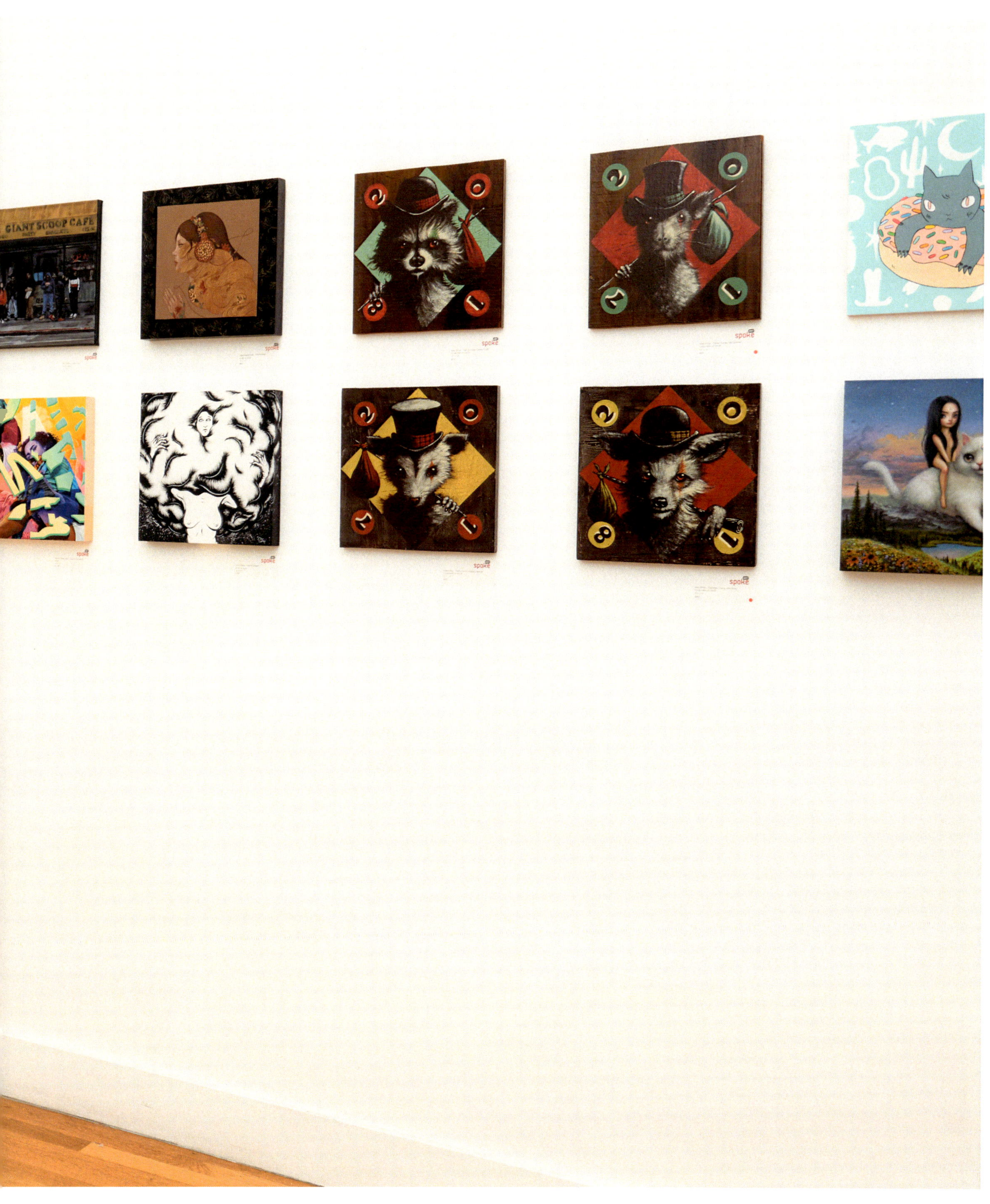

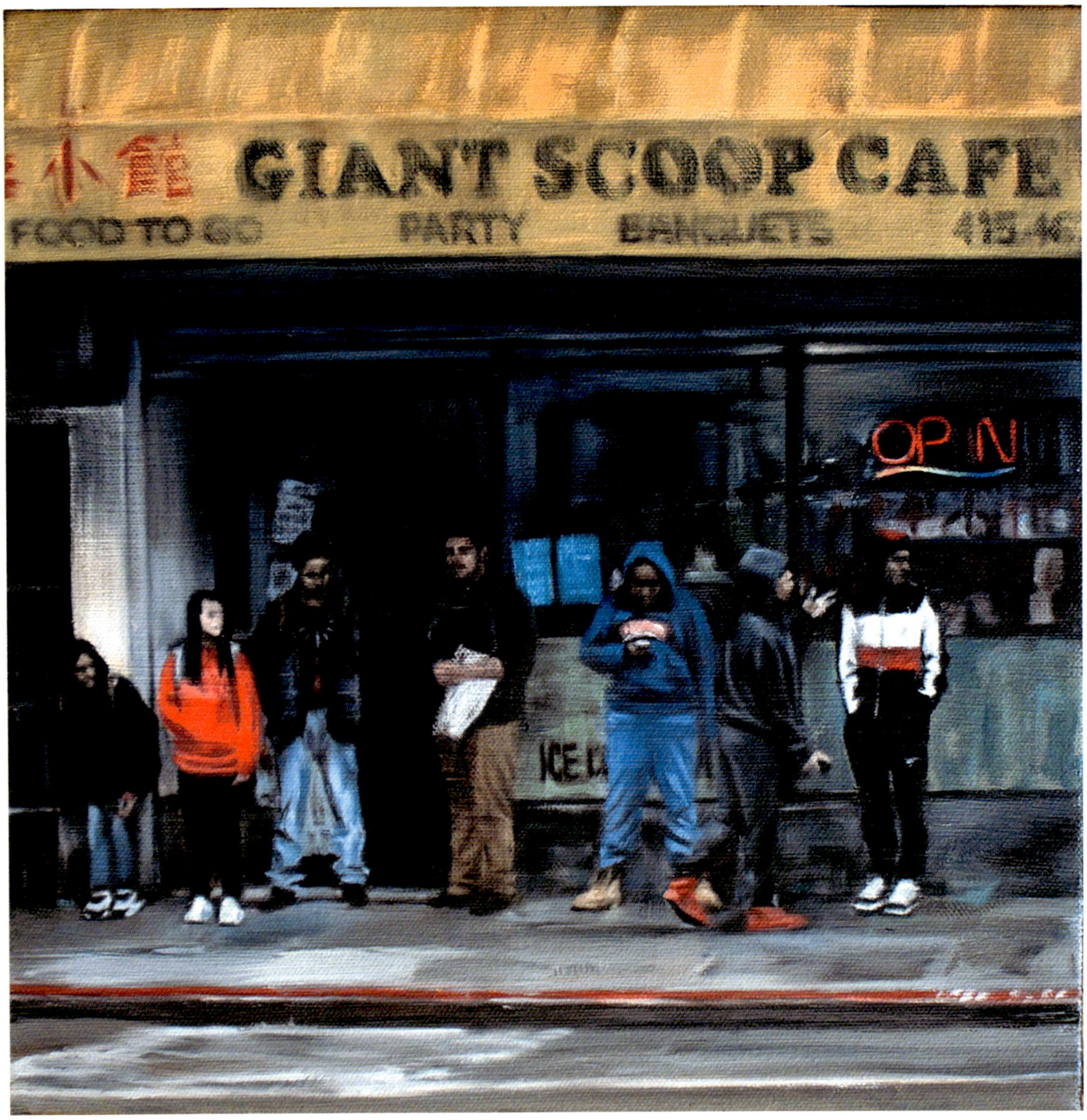

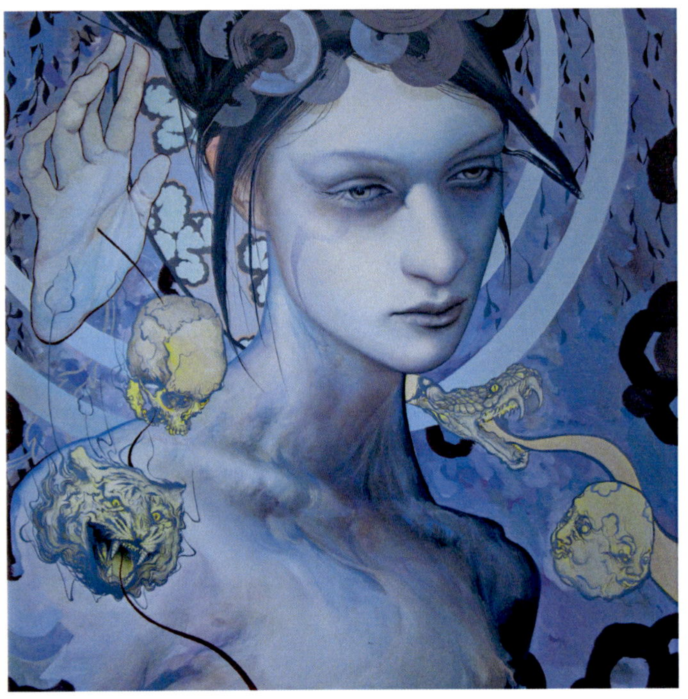

A.

B.

A. *Ryan Malley*
Giant Scoop
oil on canvas
12˝ x 12˝ (2018)

B. *Dan Quintana*
Automatic
oil on wood
12˝ x 12˝ (2018)

C. *Mwanel Pierre-Louis*
Caught in the Fields
acrylic on panel
12˝ x 12˝ (2018)

D. *Mike Shine*
Dominek, Carny Hobo Fox
house paint on wood
12˝ x 12˝ (2018)

E. *Susannah Kelly*
Inescapable
graphite on paper
12˝ x 12˝ (2018)

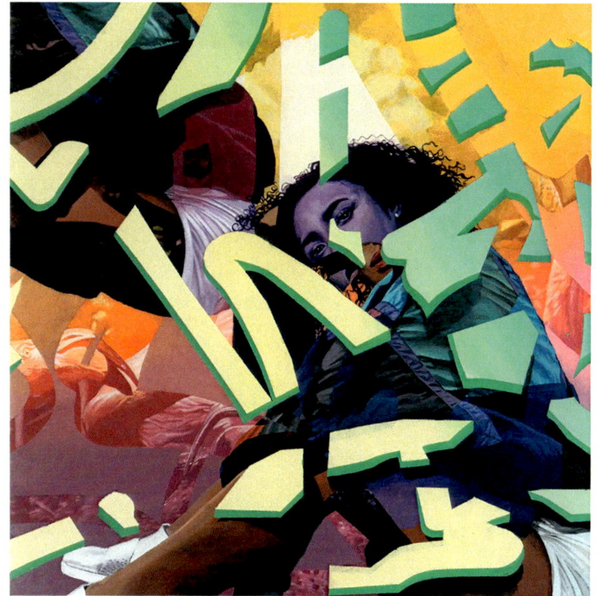

C.

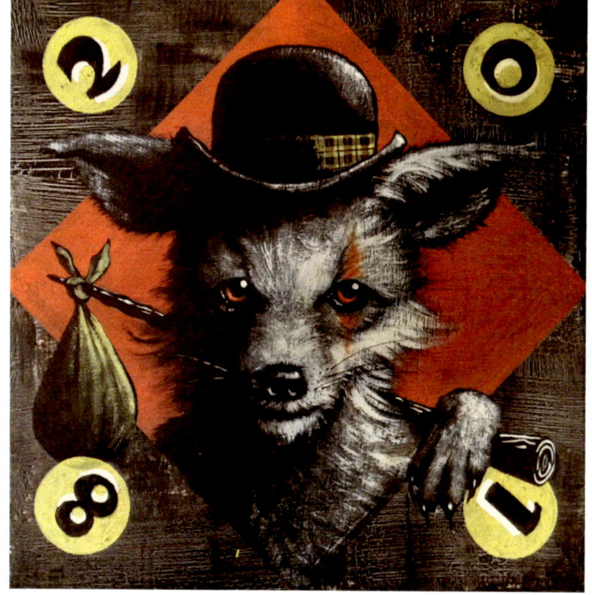

D.

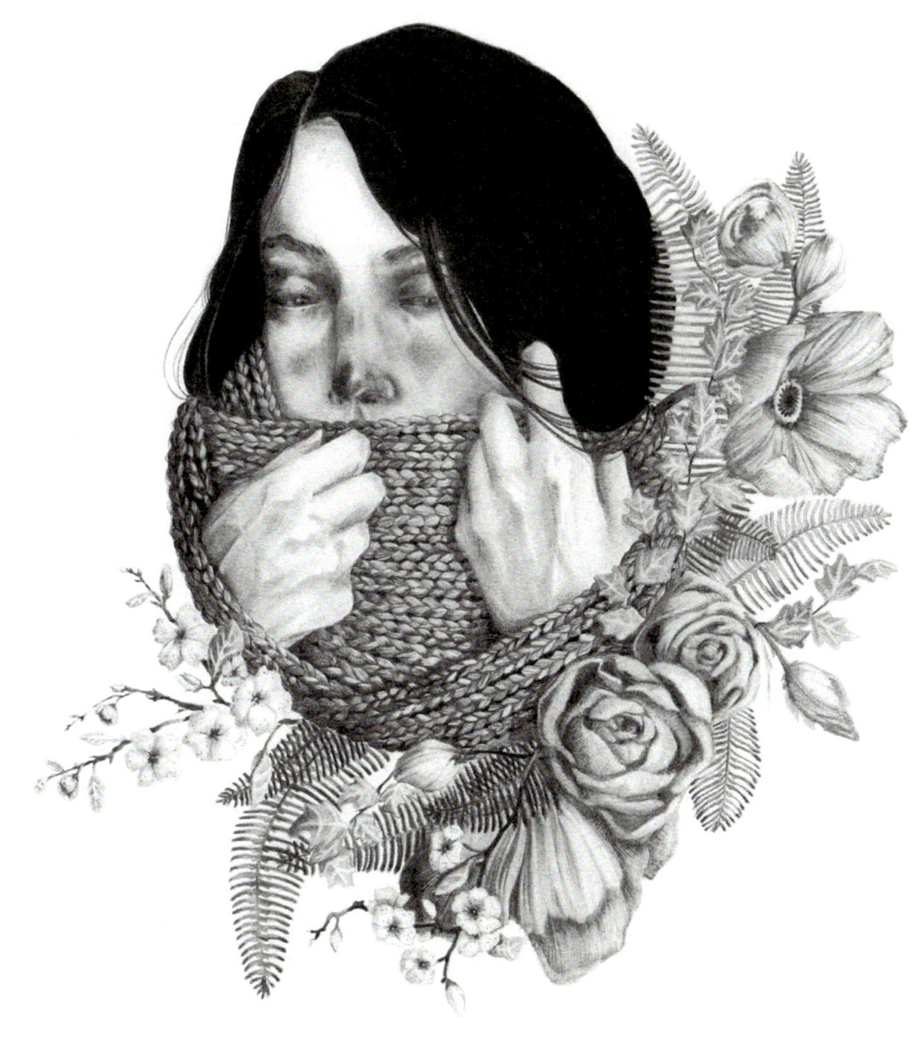

E.

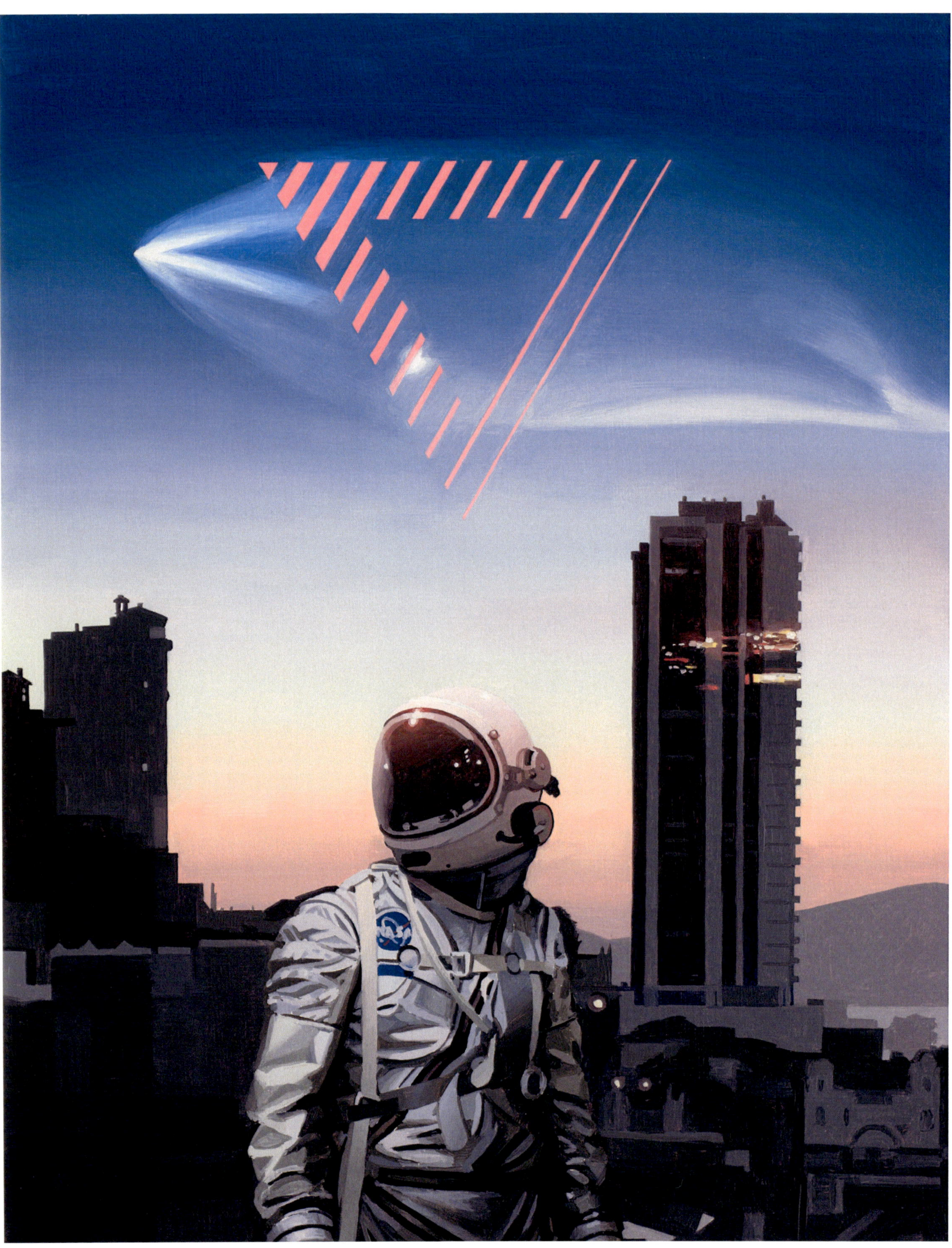

Algorithm

Scott Listfield

June 2—23
2018

Spoke Art San Francisco is pleased to present *ALGORITHM*, a solo exhibition by Massachusetts-based painter *Scott Listfield*. The new series continues the saga of Listfield's central protagonist, a lone astronaut navigating the post-apocalyptic landscape of San Francisco and Silicon Valley.

Listfield's latest body of oil paintings are set in a world populated by drones, self-driving vehicles, and robots. The work presents a derelict aftermath, inviting the view to consider a cityscape overrun by technology and devoid of human life.

The work is critical of the ways in which we interface with an ever-changing technological landscape. Examining this pivotal moment in time, Listfield ponders, *"Just because we can do something, does that mean we should? What is technology without the human component? And what kind of problems are we solving?"*

Scott Listfield

Space X

oil on canvas
20″ x 16″ (2018)

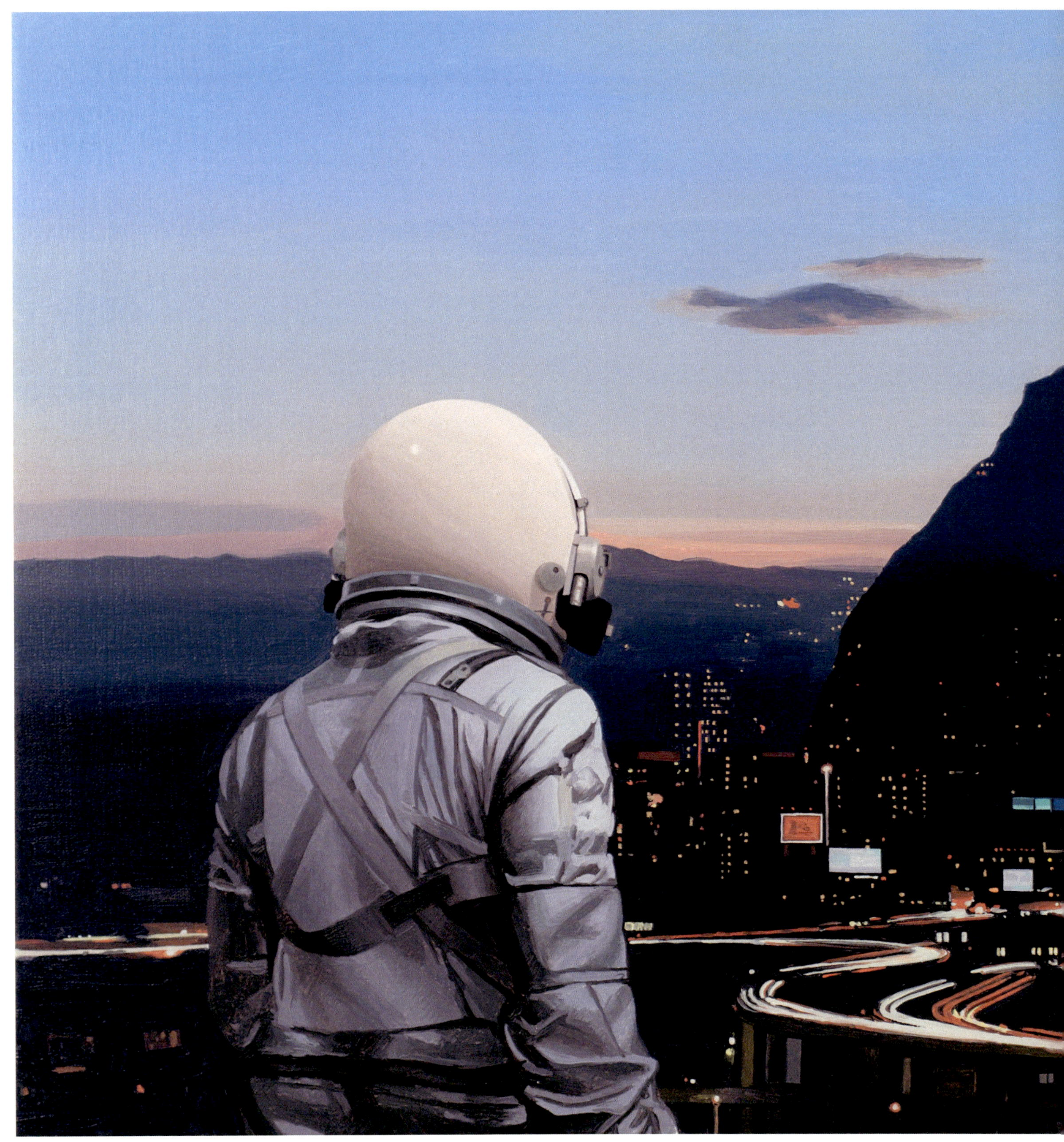

Sun Sets on The City

oil on canvas
20˝ x 40˝ (2018)

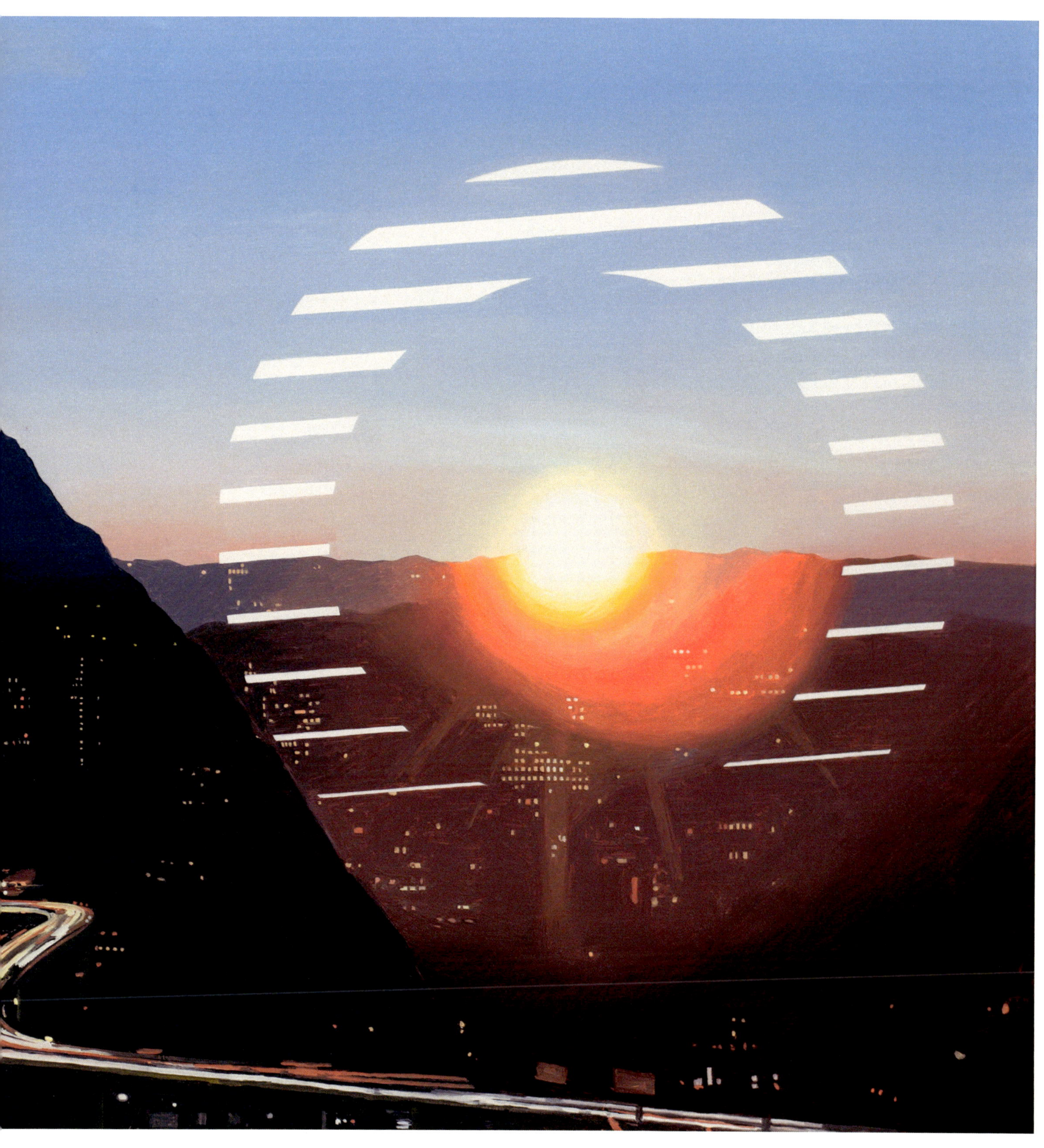

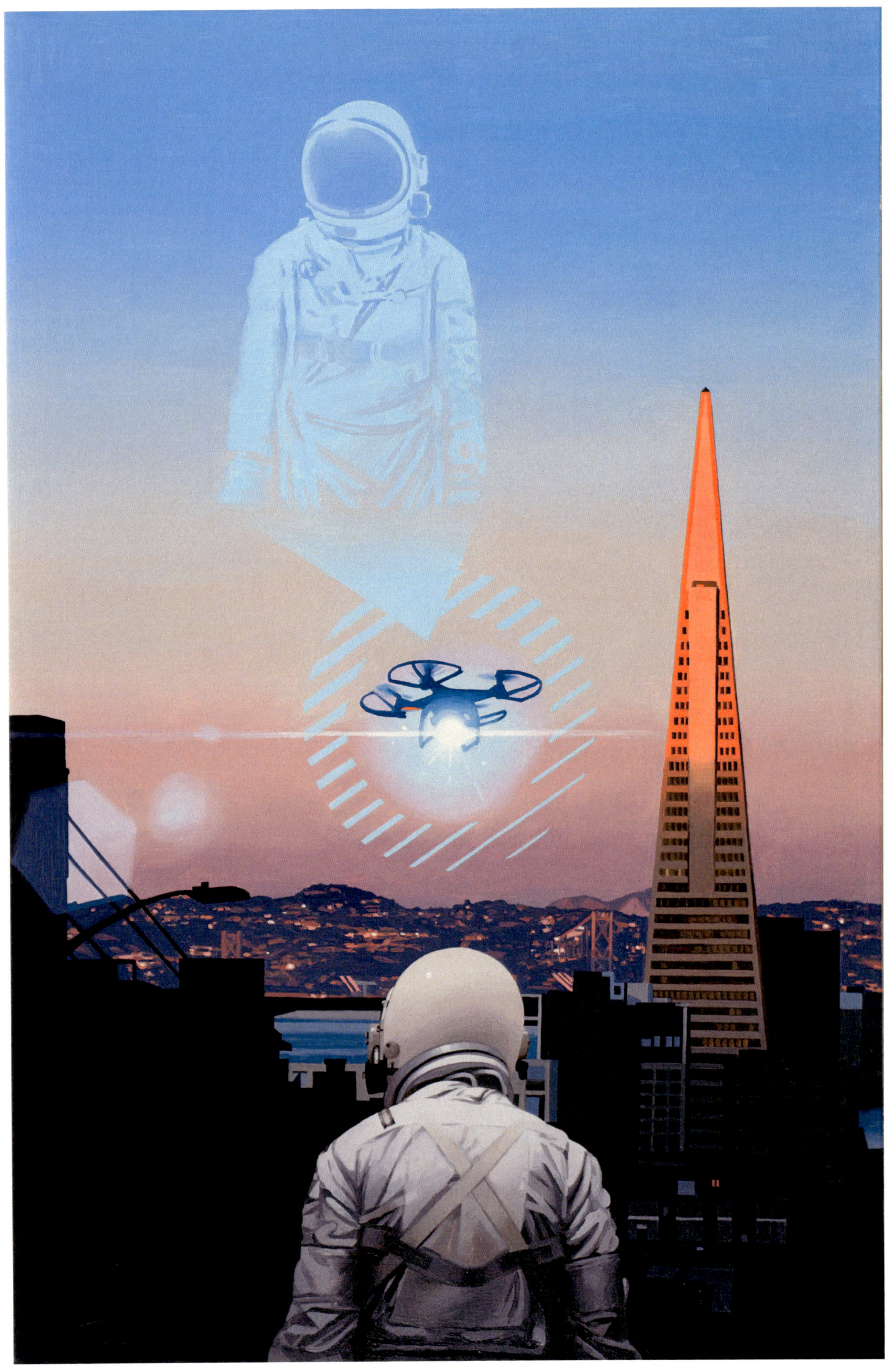

A.

B.

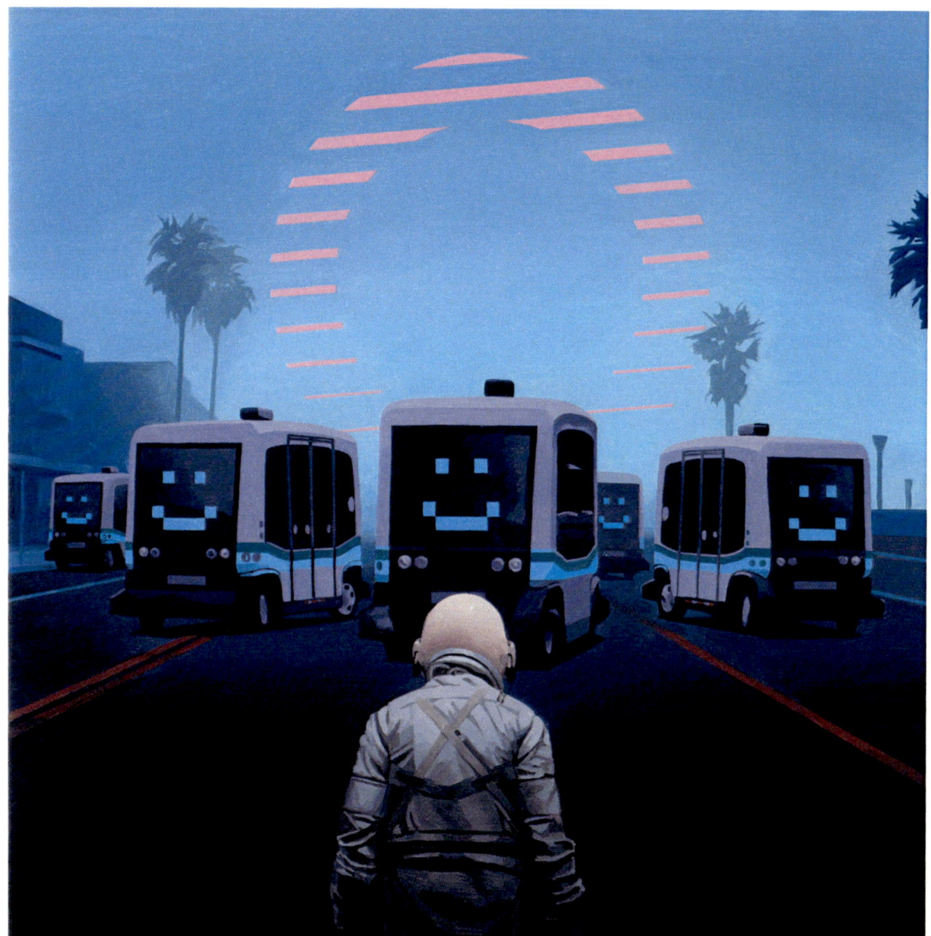

C.

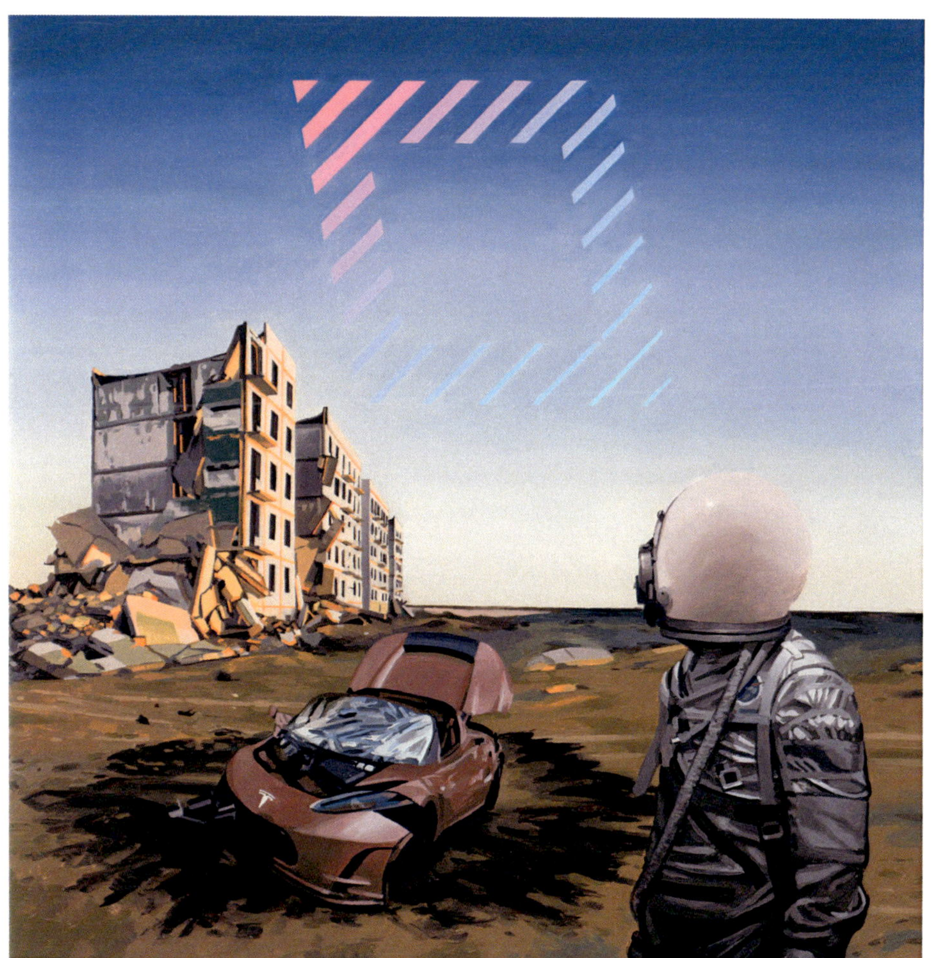

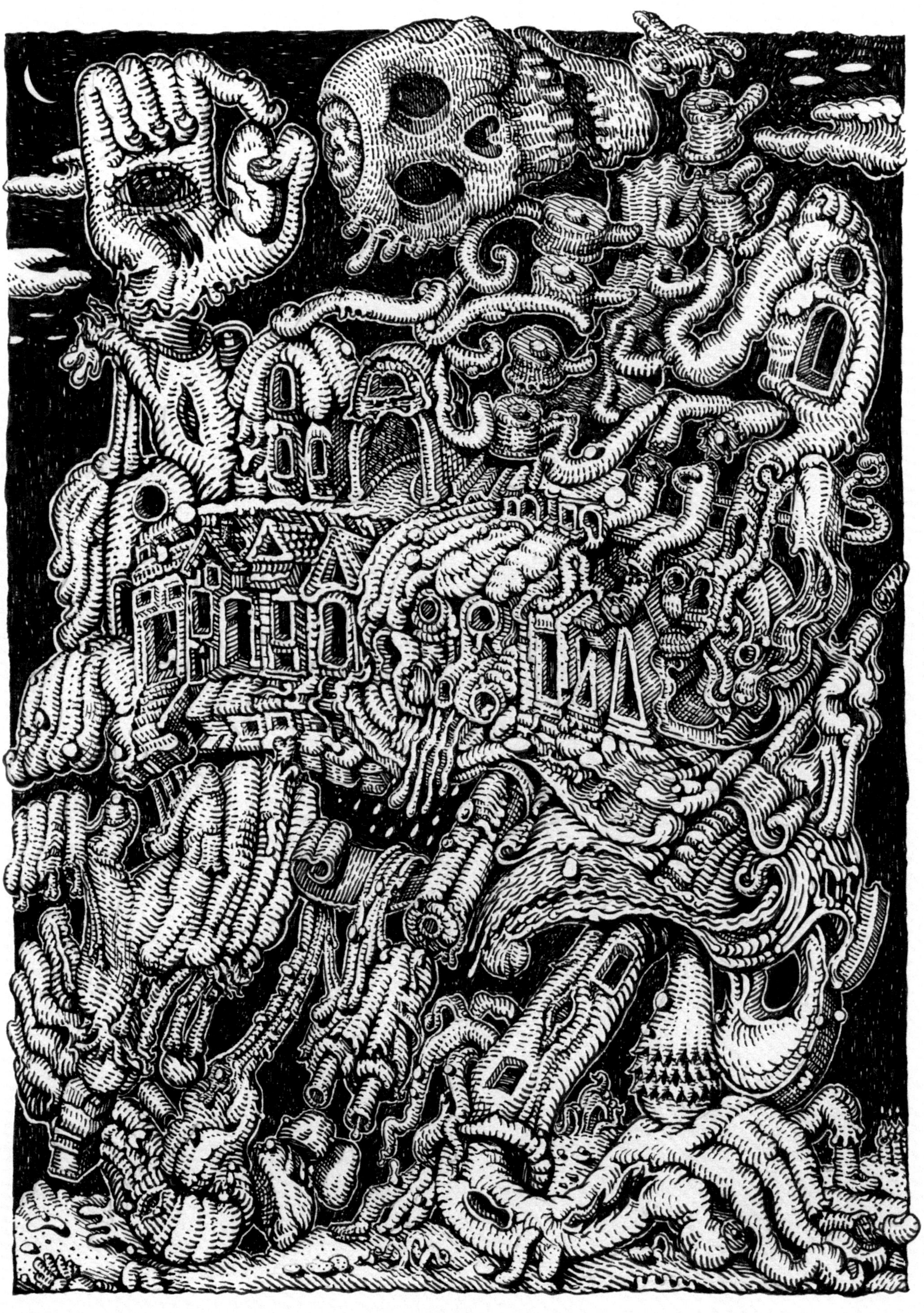

Under the Marquee

David Welker

July 7—28
2018

Spoke Art San Francisco is pleased to present **Under the Marquee**, a solo exhibition by acclaimed New York-based artist and illustrator **David Welker**. For his second solo show with the gallery, Welker has employed his signature style to continue the ongoing narrative held within the peculiar world of his work.

The dense ink drawings created for Under the Marquee explore nature blending with man-made architecture. Drawn to the theatre marquee as a beacon and gathering place, Welker's abstracted lettering and signage figure prominently in the new body of work, though never (and intentionally) fully revealing the mystic message within.

The veiled narrative of David's latest take the viewer on a psychedelic journey to castles by the sea, improbable anthropomorphized structures, tranquil landscapes, and beyond. Welker describes the brimming abstracted forms as "*mutated theatrical marquees*" that seem to shift and reveal themselves with each examination.

David Welker
The Disassembled Man
ink on paper
9″ x 12″ (2018)

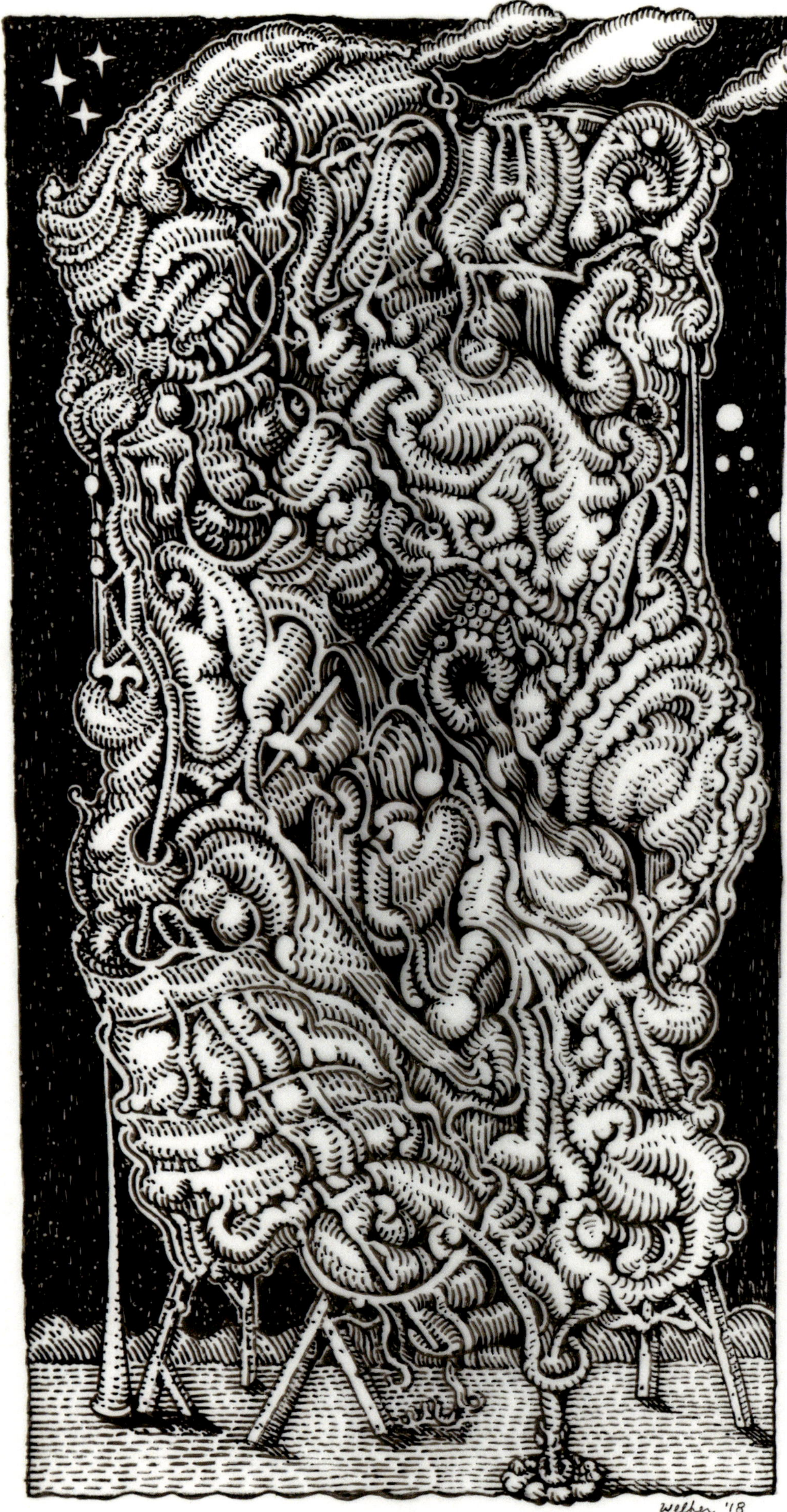

A. *David Welker*

The Ventrilaquist's Suitcase
pen and ink on vellum
6˝ x 10 ¾˝ (2018)

B. *David Welker*

The Aqueduct
pen on vellum
6½˝ x 9˝ (2018)

C. *David Welker*

The Flying Fish
pen on vellum
4¼˝ x 4¼˝ (2018)

D. *David Welker*

The Maze Skull
pen on vellum
5¼˝ x 5¼˝ (2018)

A.

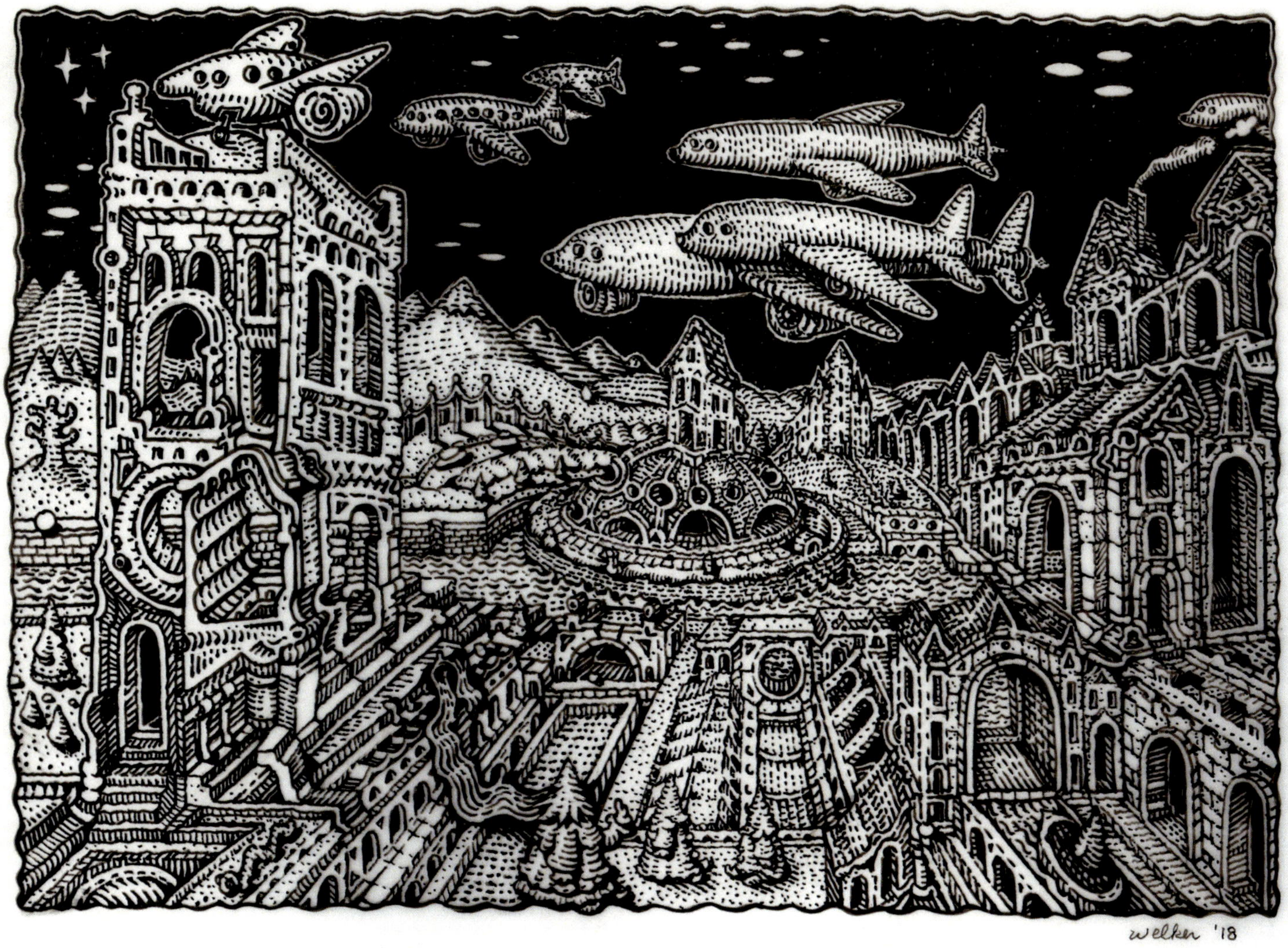

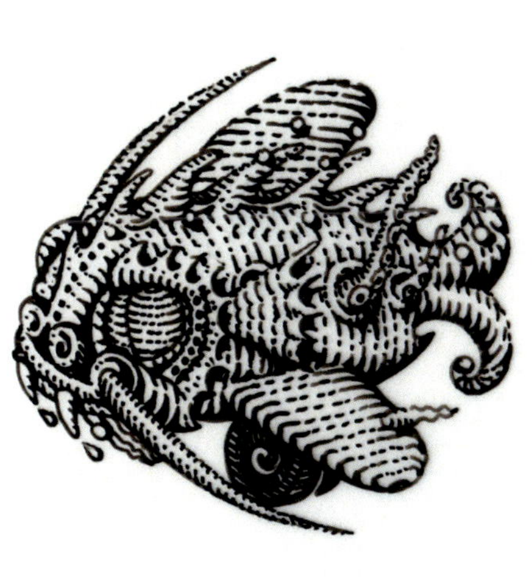

C.

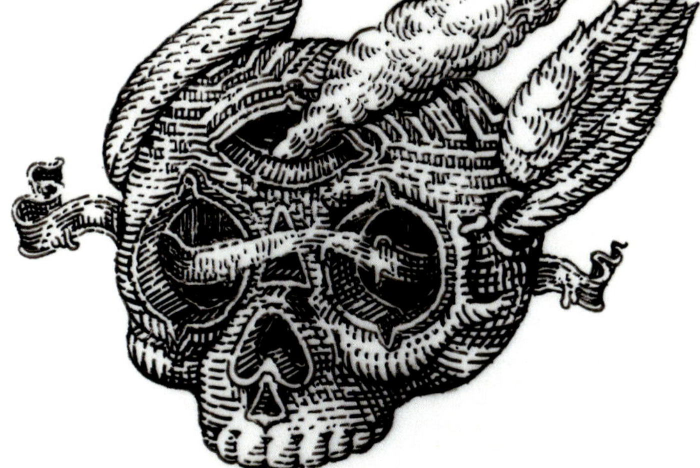

D.

B.

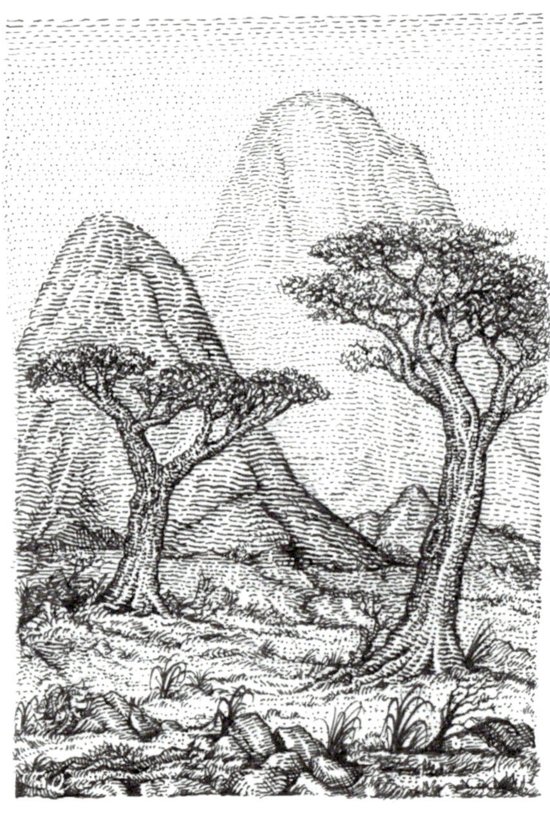

The Savannah
pen on Stonehenge paper
5˝ x 7˝ (2018)

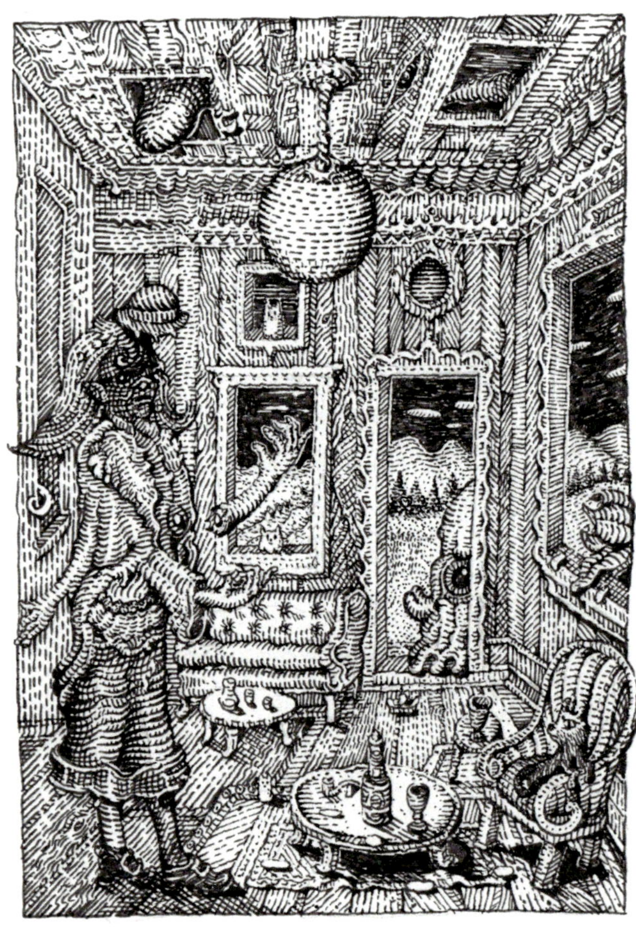

Tea at Aunt Susie's House
pen on Stonehenge paper
5˝ x 7˝ (2018)

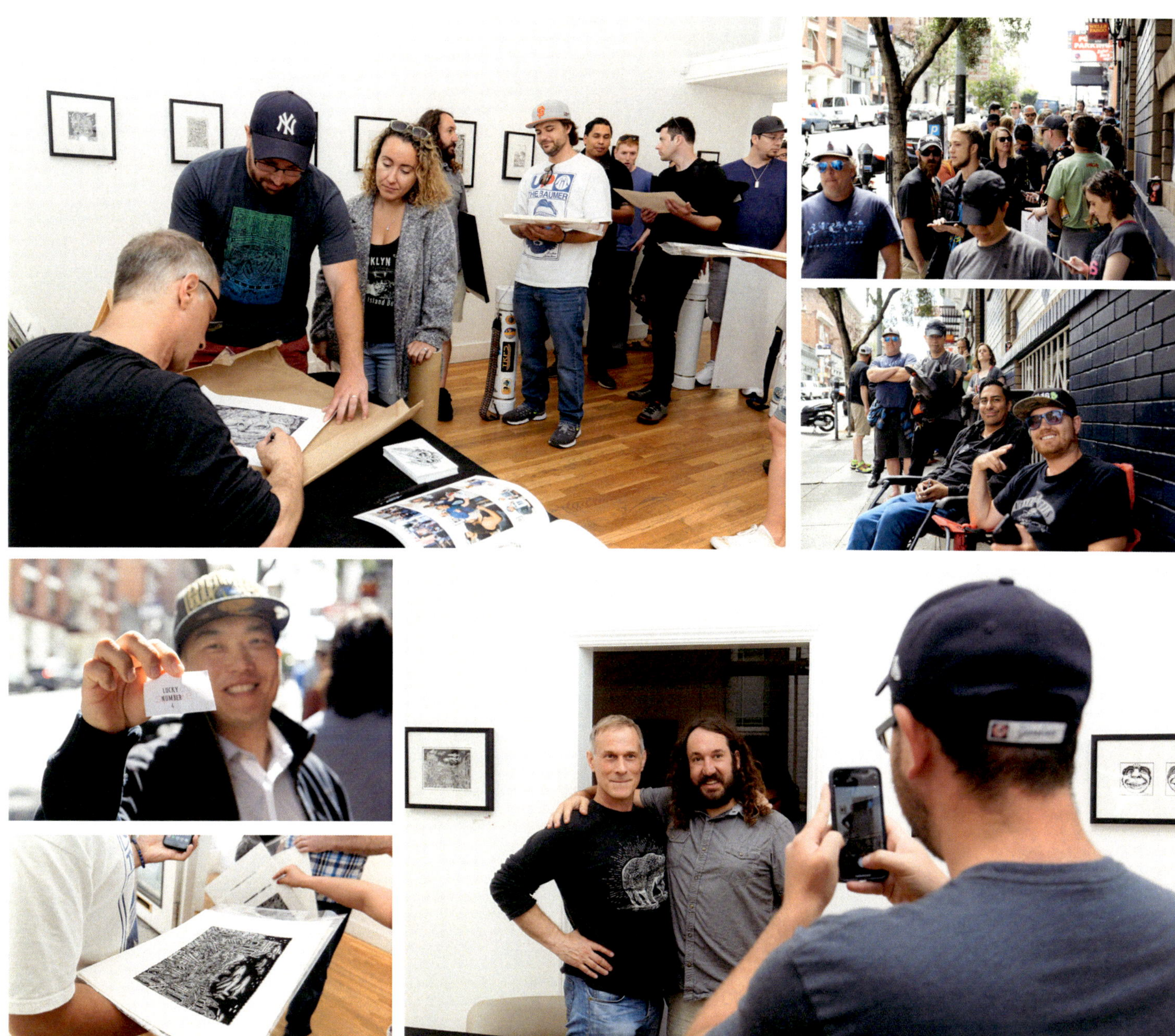

Opening Reception

PHOTOS: Shaun Roberts

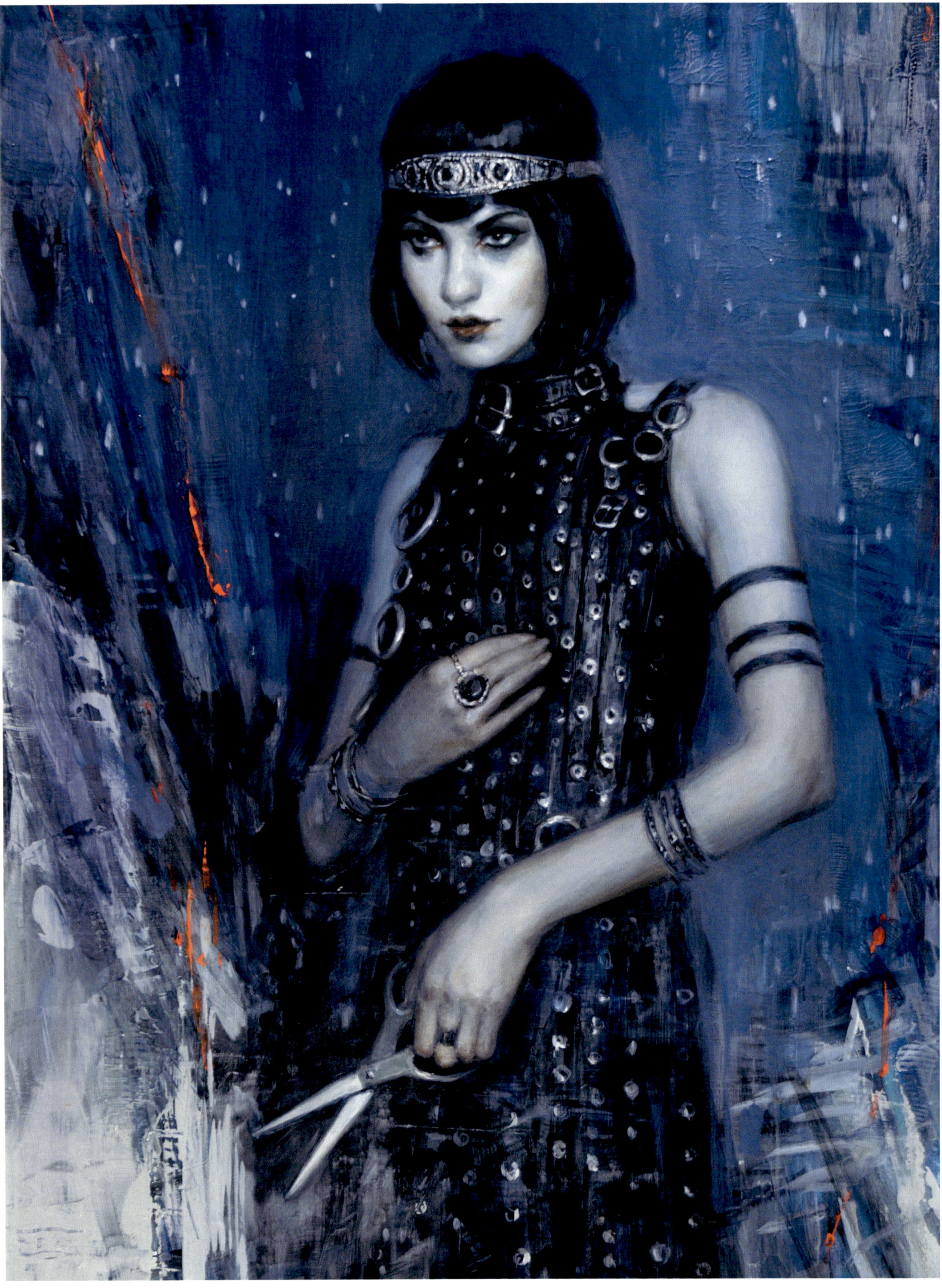

Lukomorye

Nadezda

Spoke Art San Francisco is pleased to present *Lukomorye*, a solo exhibition by Bay Area-based painter *Nadezda*. For her inaugural solo exhibition with the gallery, she has created a body of new work that take the viewer on a fantastical journey to a world of romantic, dark fairytales teeming with hidden mysteries.

Influenced by Russian folklore, children's stories, theatre, and beyond, Nadezda's masterfully executed oil paintings and graphite drawings explore the depths of imagination. As if through a delicate and impassioned dance, the artist's mark-making is full of movement illuminating figures and their environments. Balancing finely rendered details with brevity and the suggestion of narrative clues, one is left to continue the story held within each piece.

The artist invites us into the boundless depths of her creative well, where characters come creeping, gamboling and raging forth. Nadezda's work creates a sense of curiosity, at once foreboding and magnetic, sending the viewer tumbling through the magical portal contained within each frame into the land of Lukomorye.

Nadezda
Silver Cuts (detail)
oil on panel
48˝ x 24˝ (2018)

A.

B.

C.

D.

A.	*Nadezda*
Promethea
oil on panel
6″ x 6″ (2018)

B.	*Nadezda*
Black Pavane
oil on panel
8″ x 8″ (2018)

C.	*Nadezda*
Etude with
an Apple
of Youth
oil on panel
12″ x 12″ (2018)

D.	*Nadezda*
Asleep But
Not Dreaming
oil on panel
6″ x 6″ (2018)

E.	*Nadezda*
Kostroma
oil on panel
22″ x 33″ (2018)

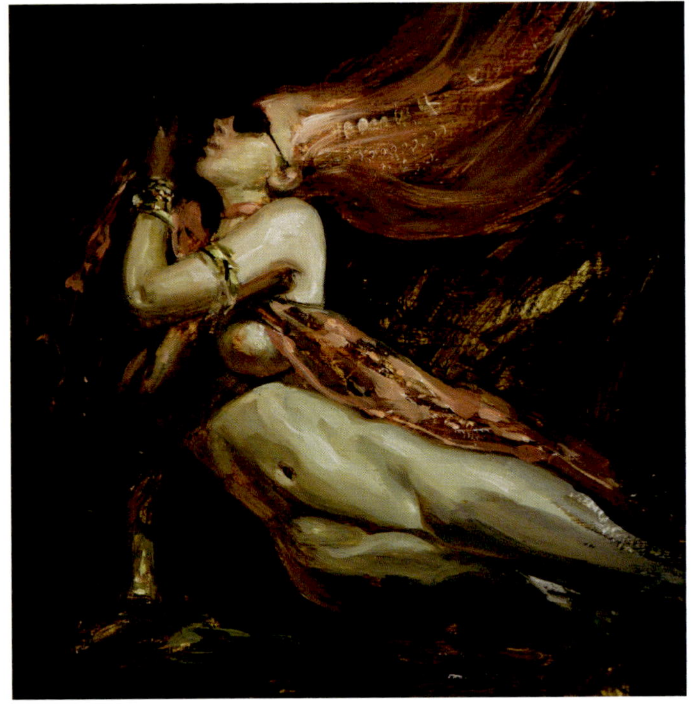

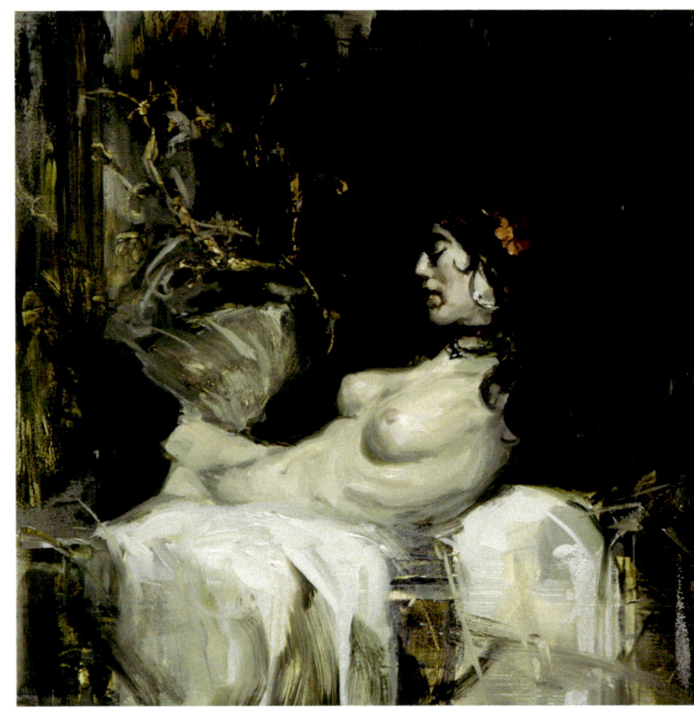

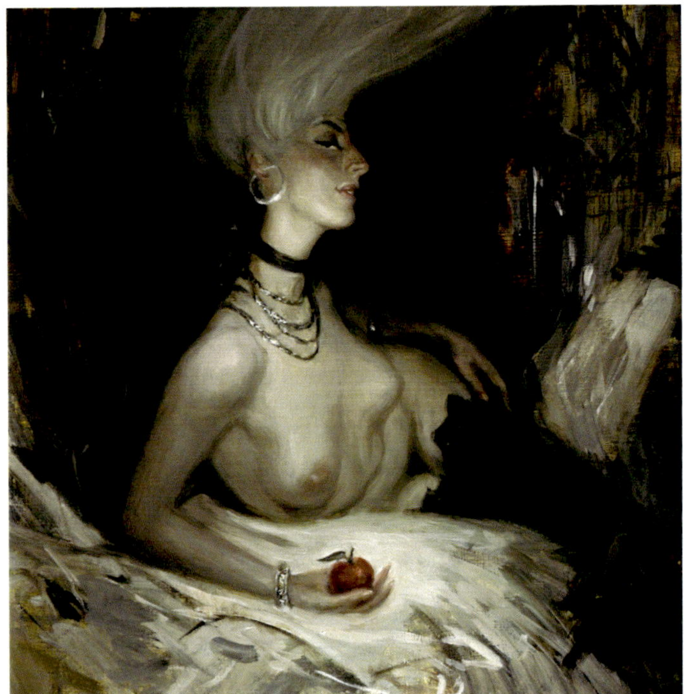

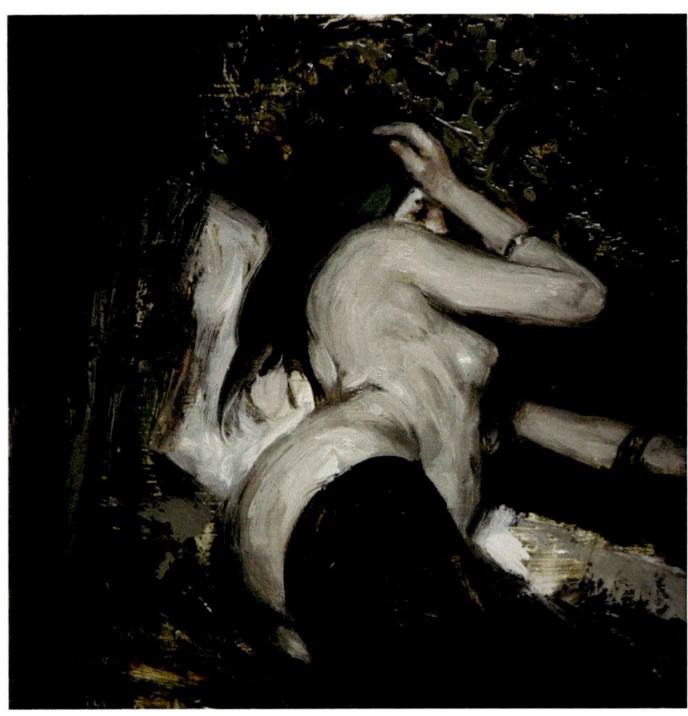

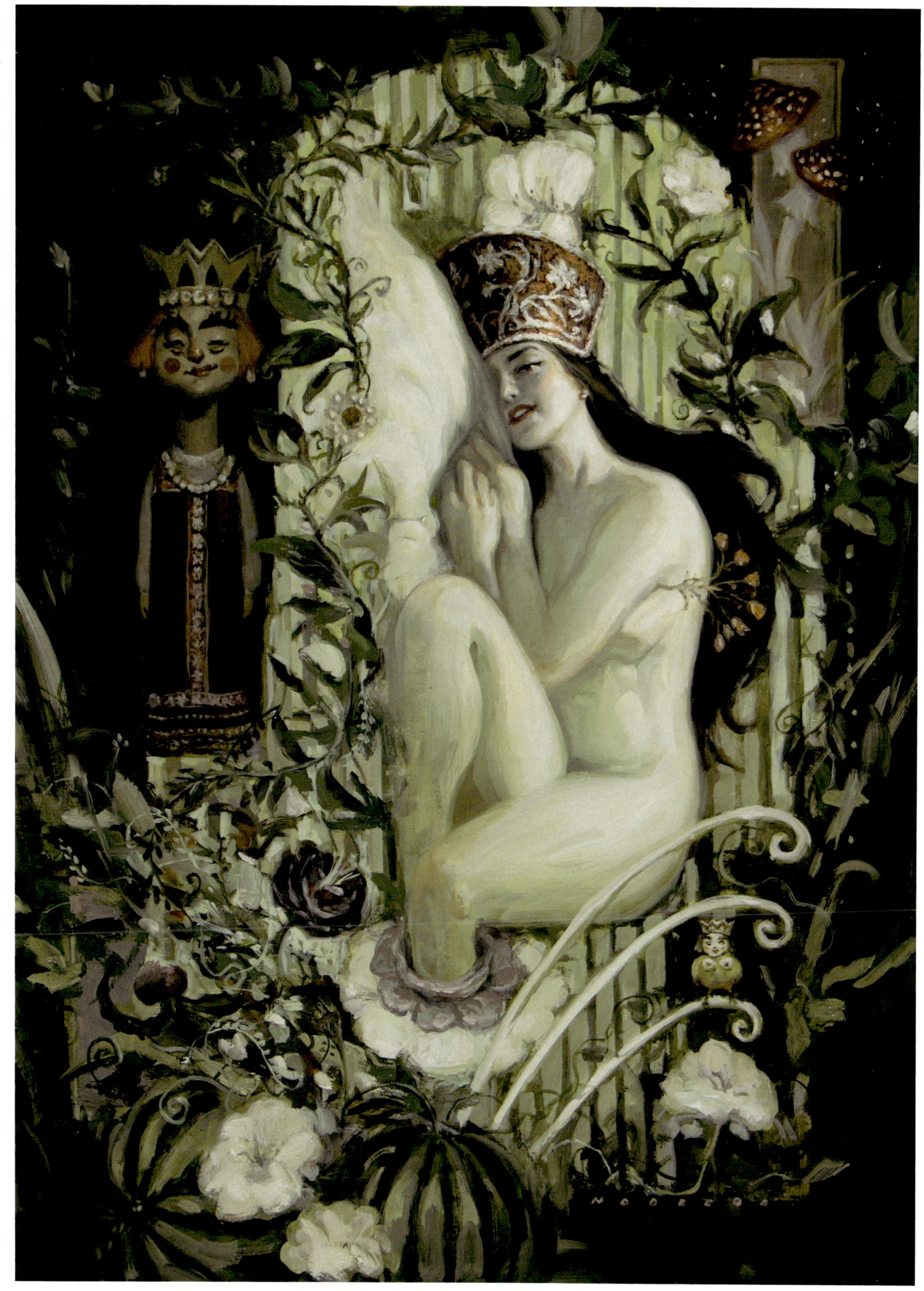

E.

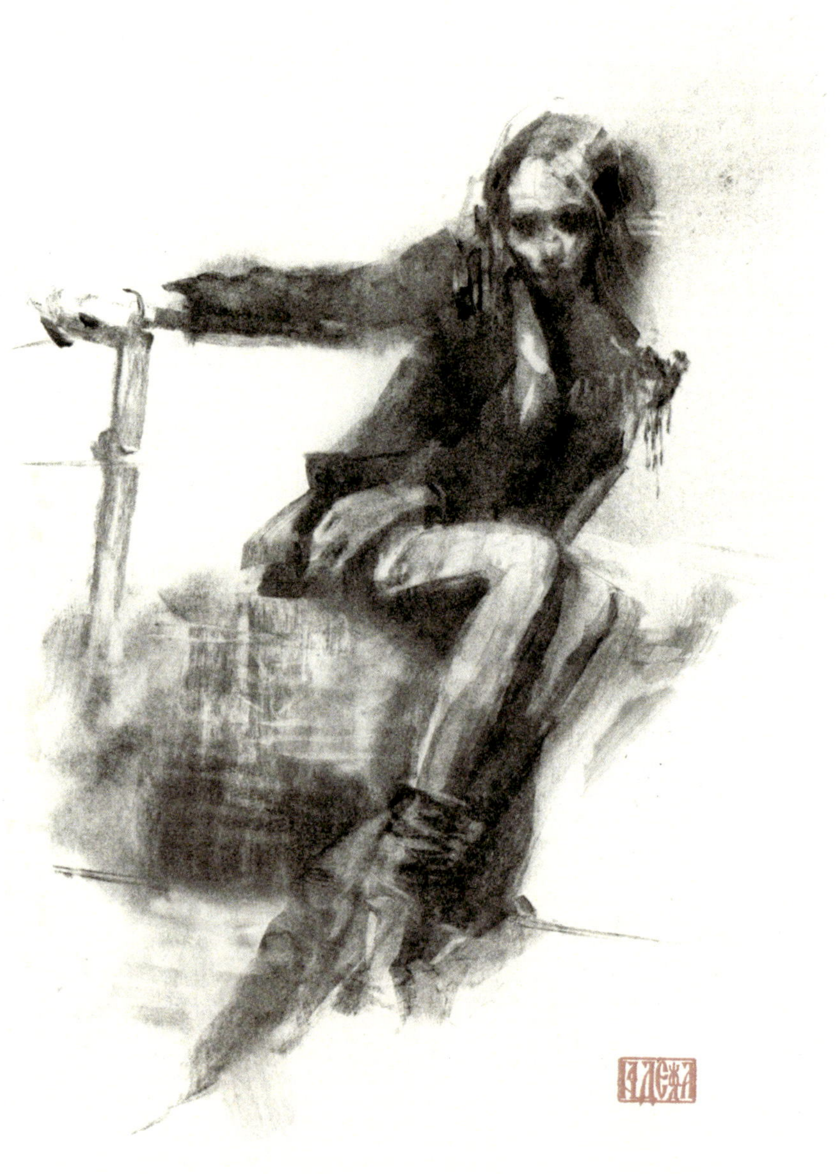

Sparrow
charcoal on paper
7˝ x 10½˝ (2018)

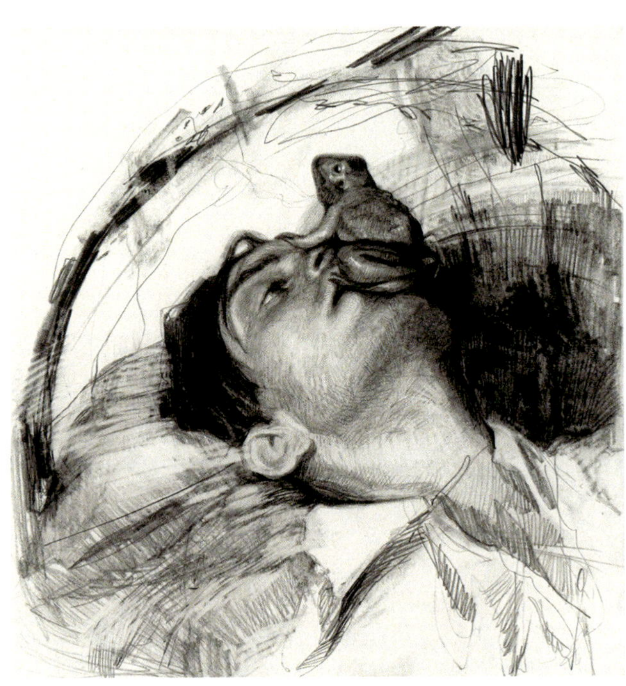

3 a.m. (study)
graphite on paper
7˝ x 7˝ (2018)

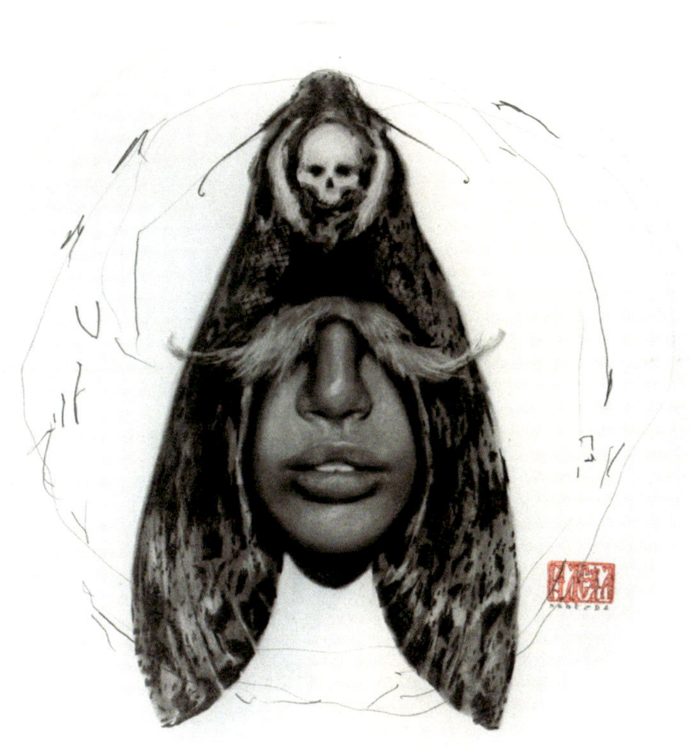

Nadezda
Kafka
graphite on paper
7½" diameter (2018)

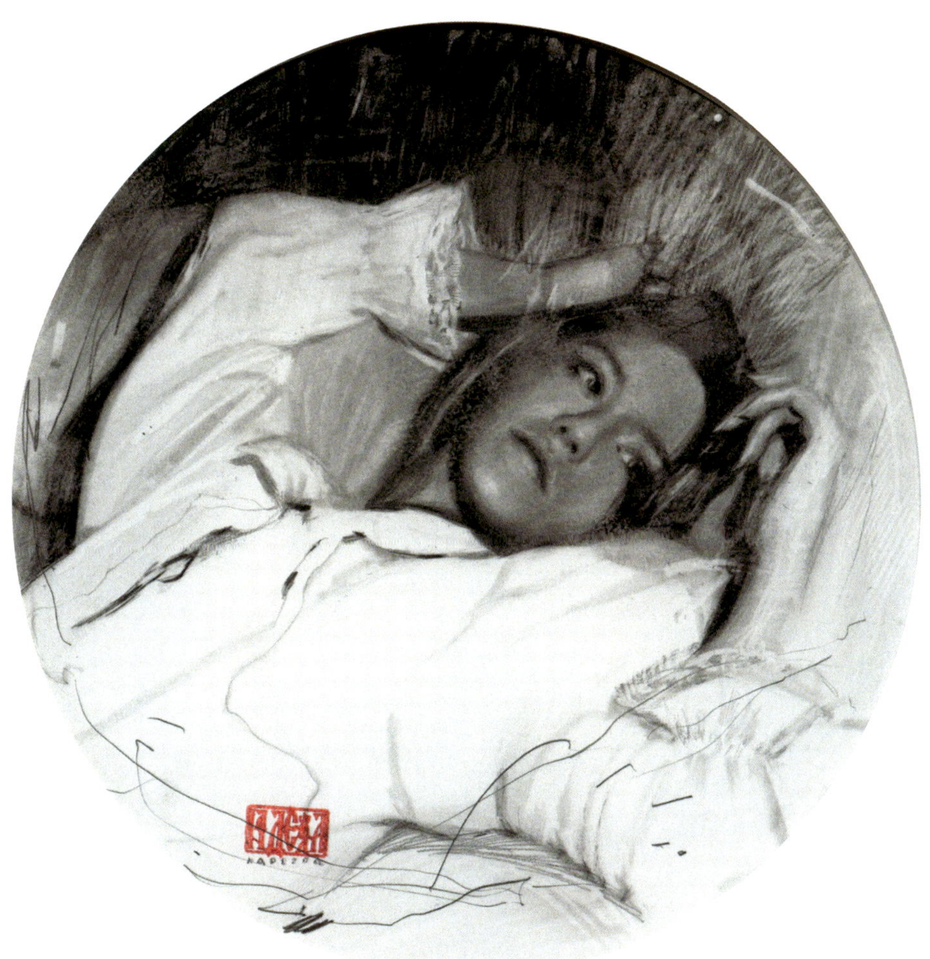

Nadezda
Juliette
graphite on paper
7½" diameter (2018)

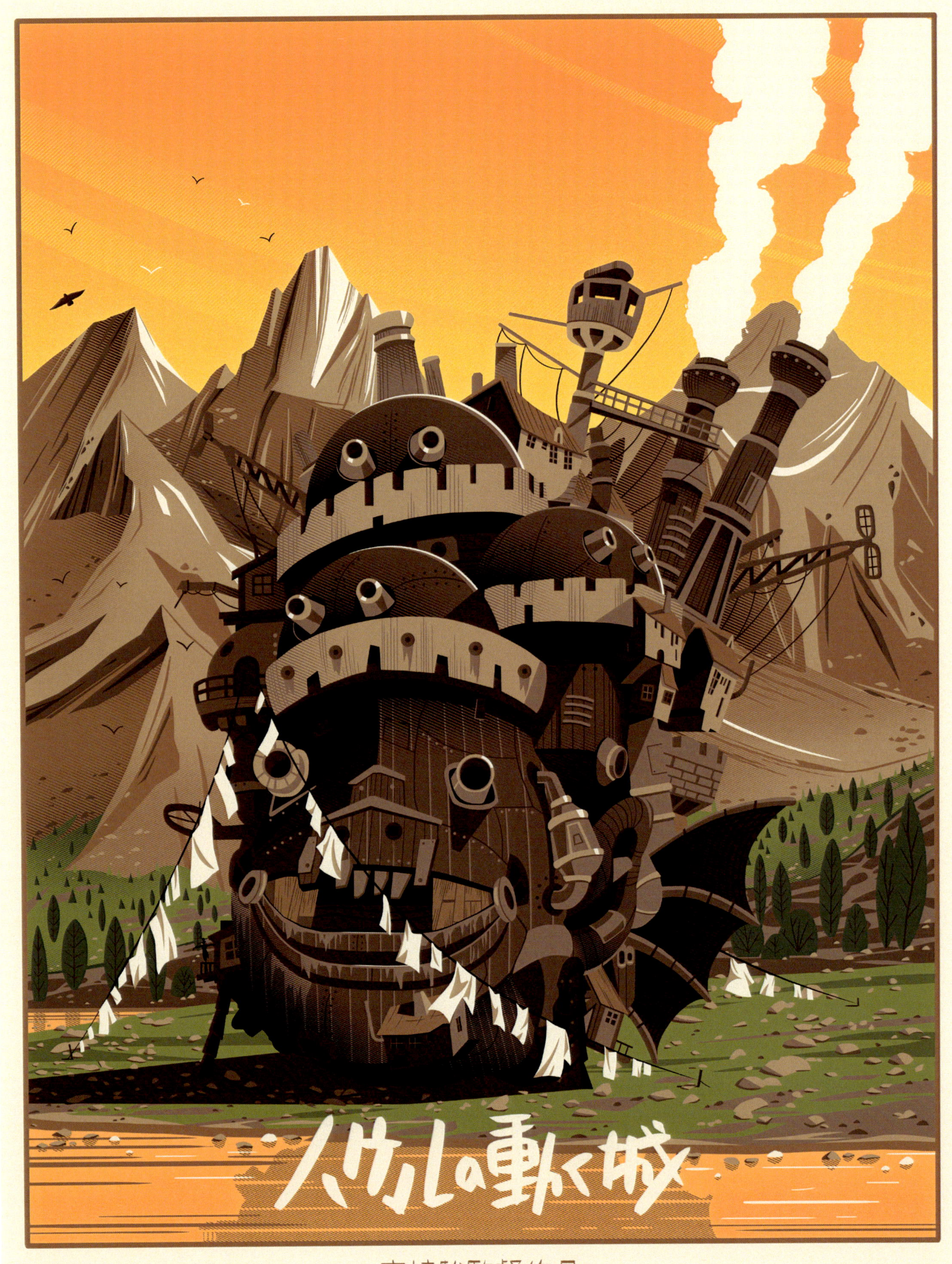

宮崎駿監督作品

Miyazaki Art Show L.A.

A Group Exhibition

SPOKE ART is pleased to present the *Miyazaki Tribute Art Show* in Los Angeles, a whimsical showcase of over 100 international artists celebrating the films of Japanese film-maker and animator Hayao Miyazaki.

Taking inspiration from the Studio Ghibli director's classic films such as My Neighbor Totoro, Kiki's Delivery Service, Porco Rosso, Howl's Moving Castle, Ponyo, The Wind Rises, Spirited Away, and Princess Mononoke, exhibiting artists have created unique works inspired by Miyazaki's imaginative universe.

Featuring a diverse array of painting, embroidery, sculpture and limited edition prints, each artist offers their unique perspective and interpretation of beloved characters and themes in Miyazaki's films. Imbued with the legendary director's sense of adventure, deep reverence for nature and strong female characters, this dynamic three day exhibition is not to be missed.

Participating Artists:

Eric Althin • Stacey Aoyama • Zard Apuya • Ana Aranda • Audra Auclair • Bagger43 • Derek Ballard • Jen Bartel • Betsy Bauer • Beau Berkley • Ryan Berkley • Laura Bifano • Blunt Graffix (Matt Dye) • Jordon Bolton • Joshua Budich • Ivonna Buenrostro • The Bungaloo • Adam Caldwell • Mar Cerdá • Elsa Chang • Alina Chau • Nomi Chi • Maggie Chiang • Tracie Ching • Charles Clary • Codeczombie • Michelle Coffee • Nick Comparone • Concepción Studios • Benjamin Constantine • Rhys Cooper • Crowded Teeth • Cuddly Rigor Mortis • Camilla d'Errico • Max Dalton • Jessica Deahl • Deangus • Mai Ly Degnan • Tim Doyle • J.M. Dragunas • Pippa Dyrlaga • Emily Dumas • James R. Eads • Kayla Edgar • Jason Edmiston • Jonathan Edwards • Tom Eglington • Felt Mistress • Freehand Profit (Gary Lockwood) • McKenzie Fisk • Ken Garduno • Monica Garwood • Sam Gilbey • James Gilleard • Sean Gillespie • Greg Gossel • Jay Gordon • Lauren Gregg • Dan Grissom • Nicole Grosjean • Justin Hagar • Evan Harris • Gina Hendry • Jed Henry • Justin Hillgrove • Kevan Hom • Scott Hopko • Primary Hughes • Alexander Iaccarino • Julia Iredale • Maggie Ivy • Candace Jean • Tim Jordan • Max Kauffman • Alex R. Kirzhner • Andrew Kolb • Jon Lau • Nan Lawson • Dustin Lincoln • Sergio Lopez • Tina Lugo • Kemi Mai • Mainger (Germain Barthelemy) • Marni Manning • Samantha Mash • Brian Mashburn • Kelly McKernan • Jose Mertz • Harry Michalakeas • Ed Mironiuk • Guillaume Morellec • JP Neang • Reuben Negron • Jeany Ngo • Chelsea O'Byrne • Karla Ortiz • Lily Padula • Colleen Palmer • Ruel Pascual • Peach MoMoKo • Minnie Phan • Kat Philbin • Ferris Plock • Primary Hughes • Raid71 • Corinne Reid • Allison Reimold • RELM • Fernando Reza • Jay Riggio • Miles Ritchie • Matt Ritchie • Em Roberts • Rebecca Rose • Sudi Rouhi • Ellie Rusinova • Yohan Sacre • Leonardo Santamaria • Charles Santoso • Valerie Savarie • Ellen Schinderman • Taylor Shultek • Chris Skinner • Kate Snow • Jessica So Ren Tang • Nick Stokes • Jason Stout • Brandan Styles • Maria Suarez-Inclan • Roland Tamayo • Anna Tillett • George Townley • Geoff Trapp • Josey Tsao • Mandy Tsung • Michael Tunk • Kelly Tunstall • Nate Utesch • Justin Van Genderen • Van Orton Design • Liz Vowles • Chris Walker • Casey Weldon • Jan Willem • Bruce Yan • Mimi Yoon • Lauren YS • Alice X Zhang • Adam Ziskie

George Townley

Howl's Moving Castle (Variant)

archival pigment print
edition of 35
24˝ x 18˝ (2018)

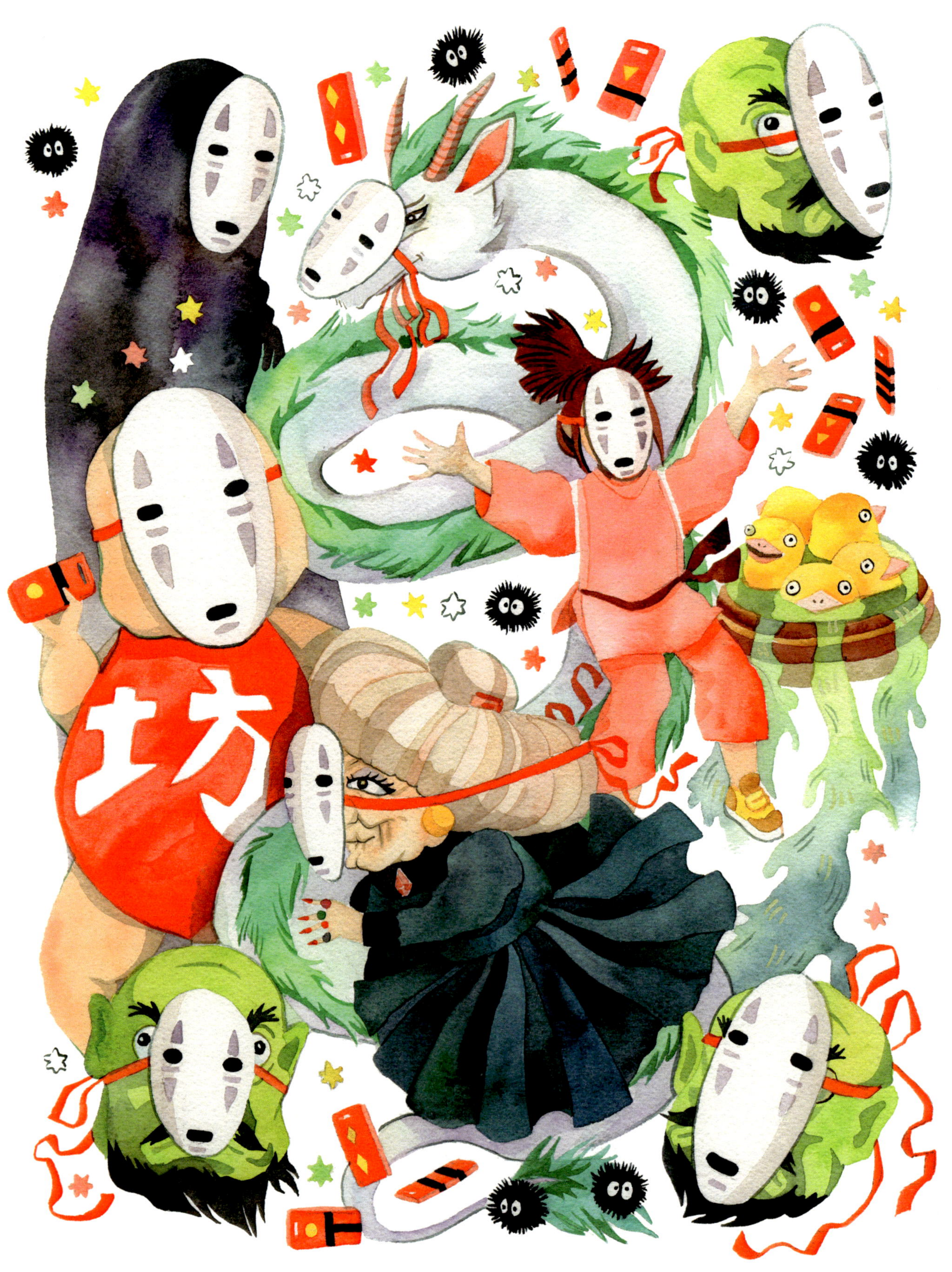

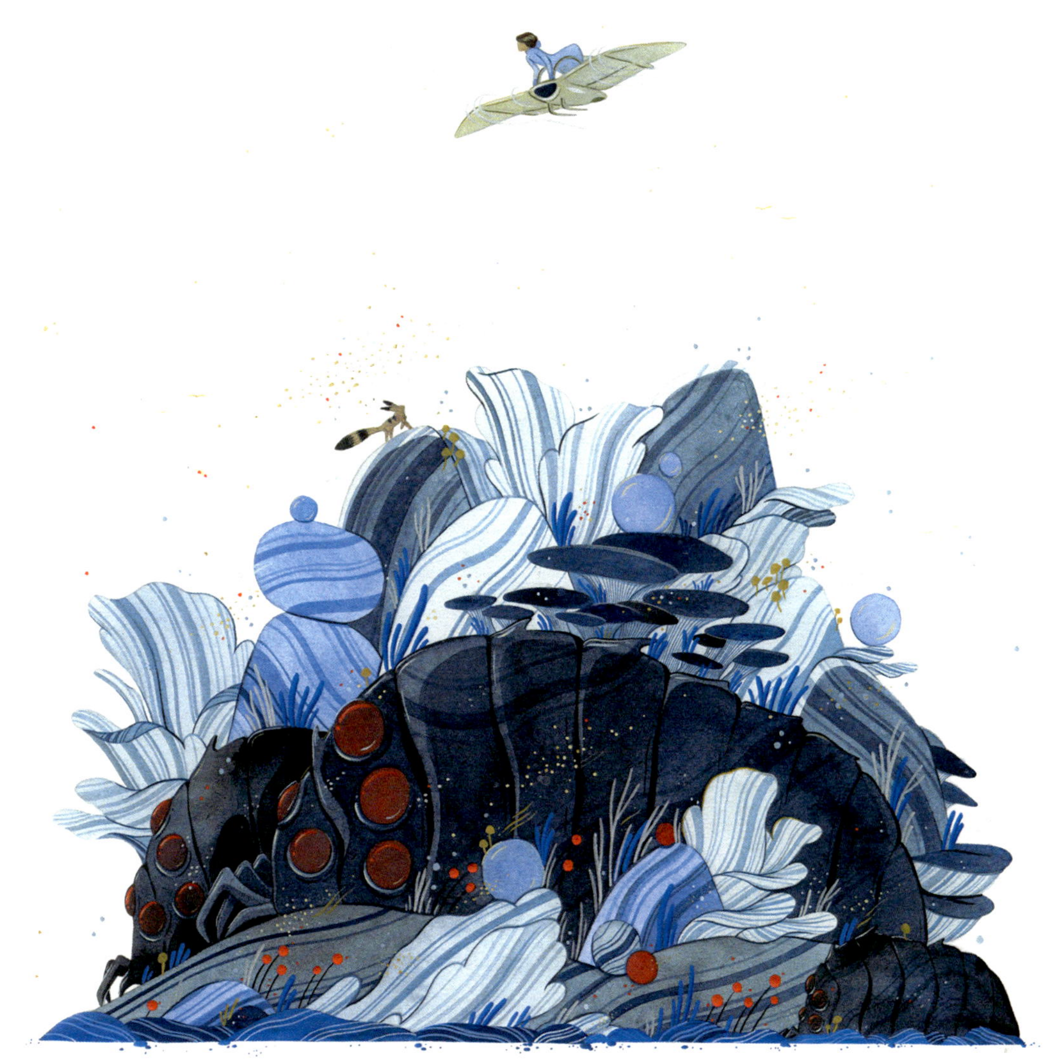

Marni Manning

No Face Fever Dream

watercolor
12" x 16" (2018)

A.

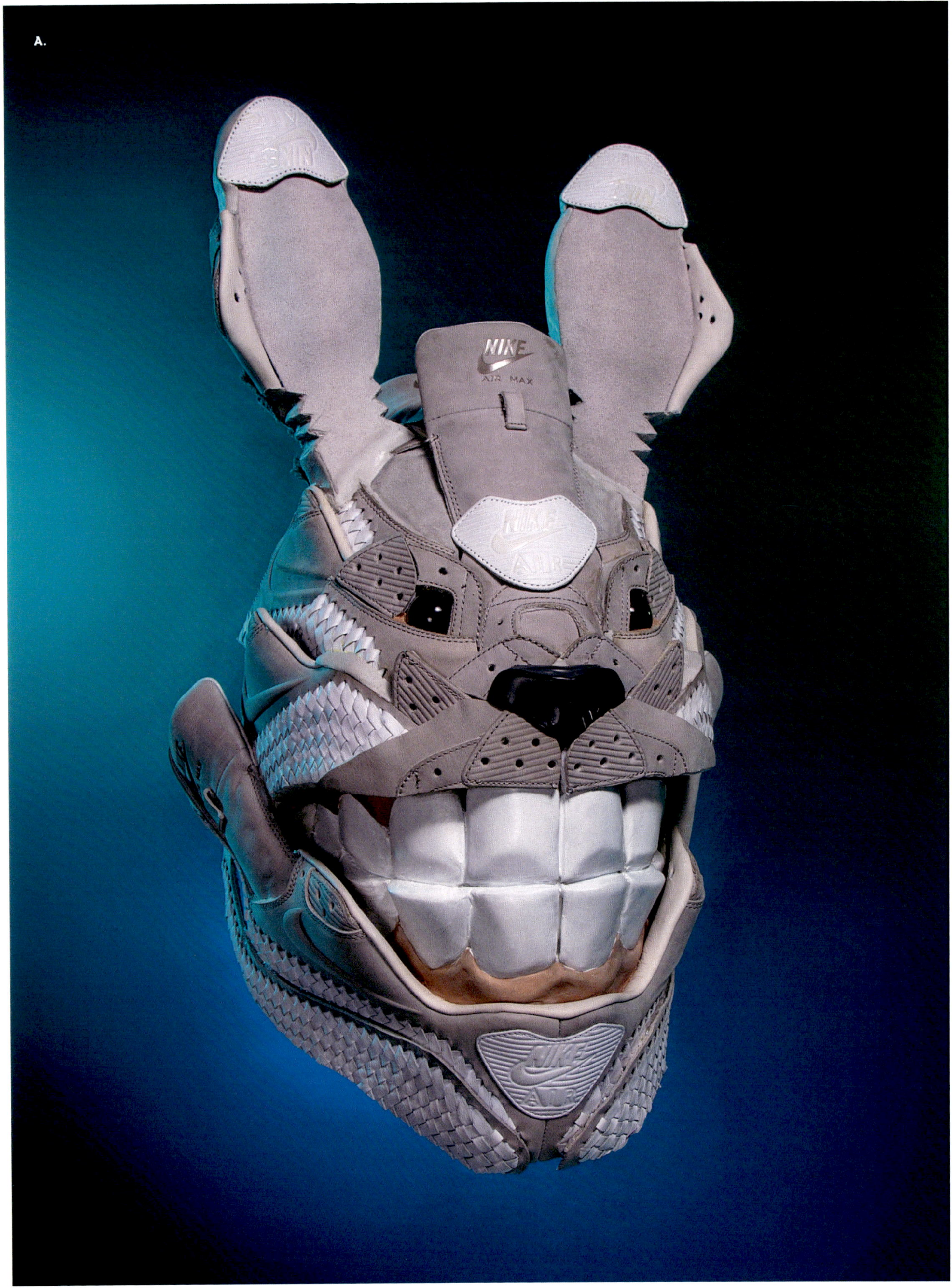

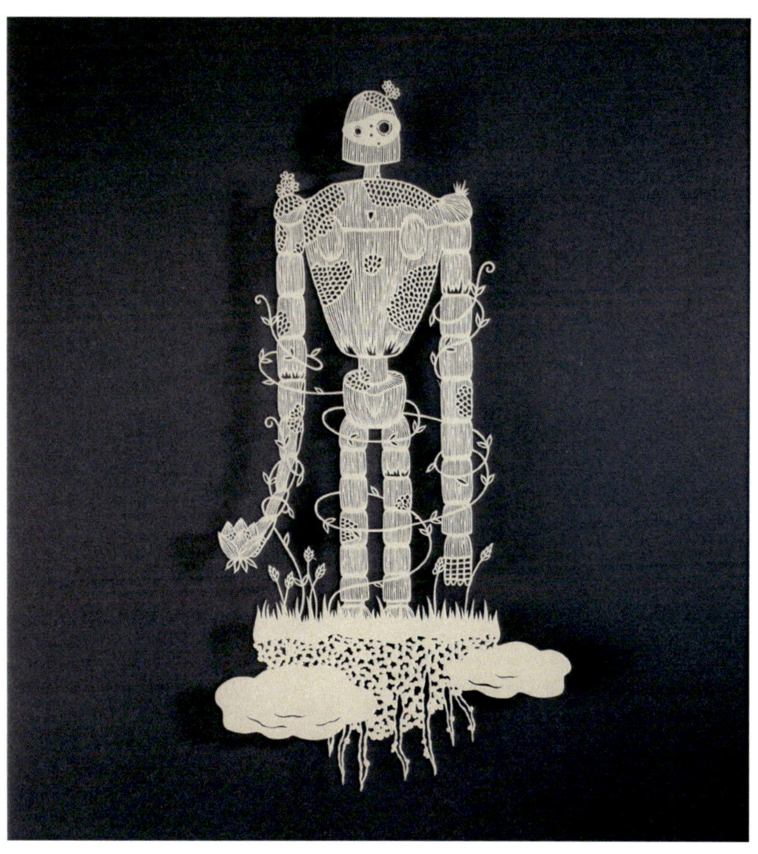

B.

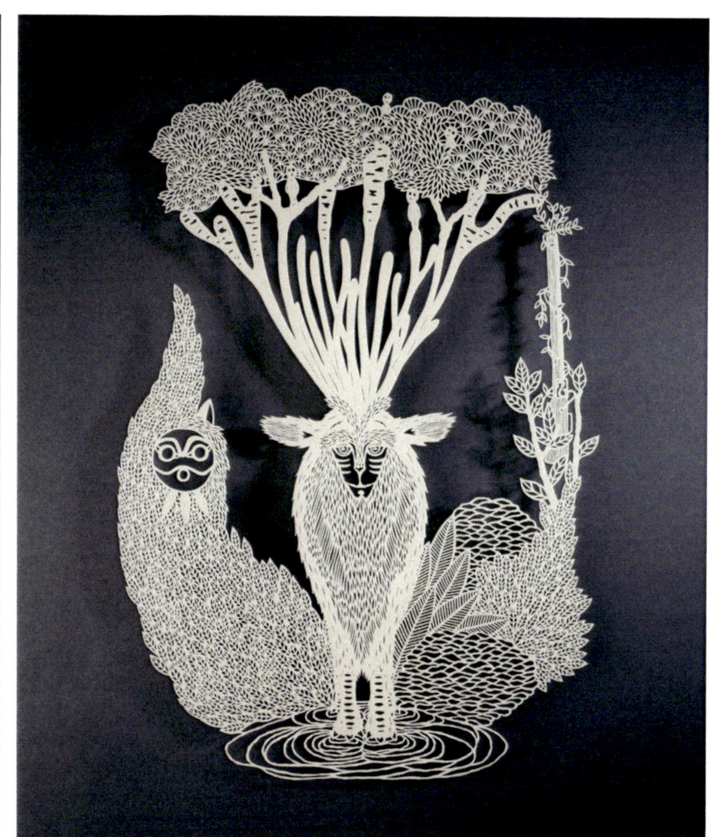

C.

A. *Freehand Profit
(Gary Lockwood)*

Totoro Air Max 90 Mask

Nike Air Max 90s, sculpting epoxy,
thermoplastic, glass eyes,
found objects
24" x 16" x 12" (2018)

B. *Pippa Dyrlaga*

The Sky Gardener

hand cut paper
6" x 10½" (2018)

C. *Pippa Dyrlaga*

The Forest Spirit

hand cut paper
8½" x 12" (2018)

D. *Eric Althin*

Greed

epoxy clay, acrylics,
and imitation gold
4" x 3½" x 4" (2018)

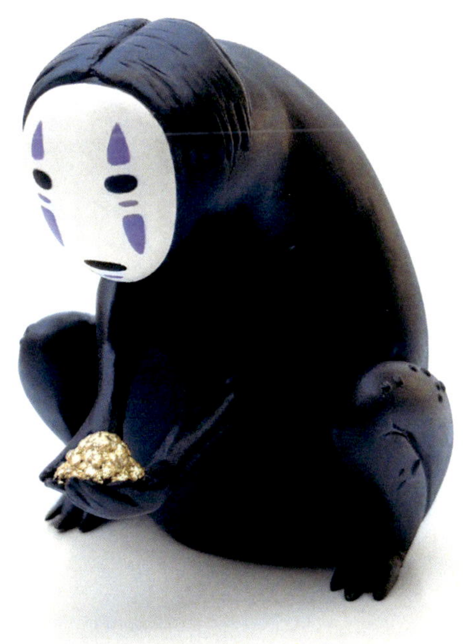

D.

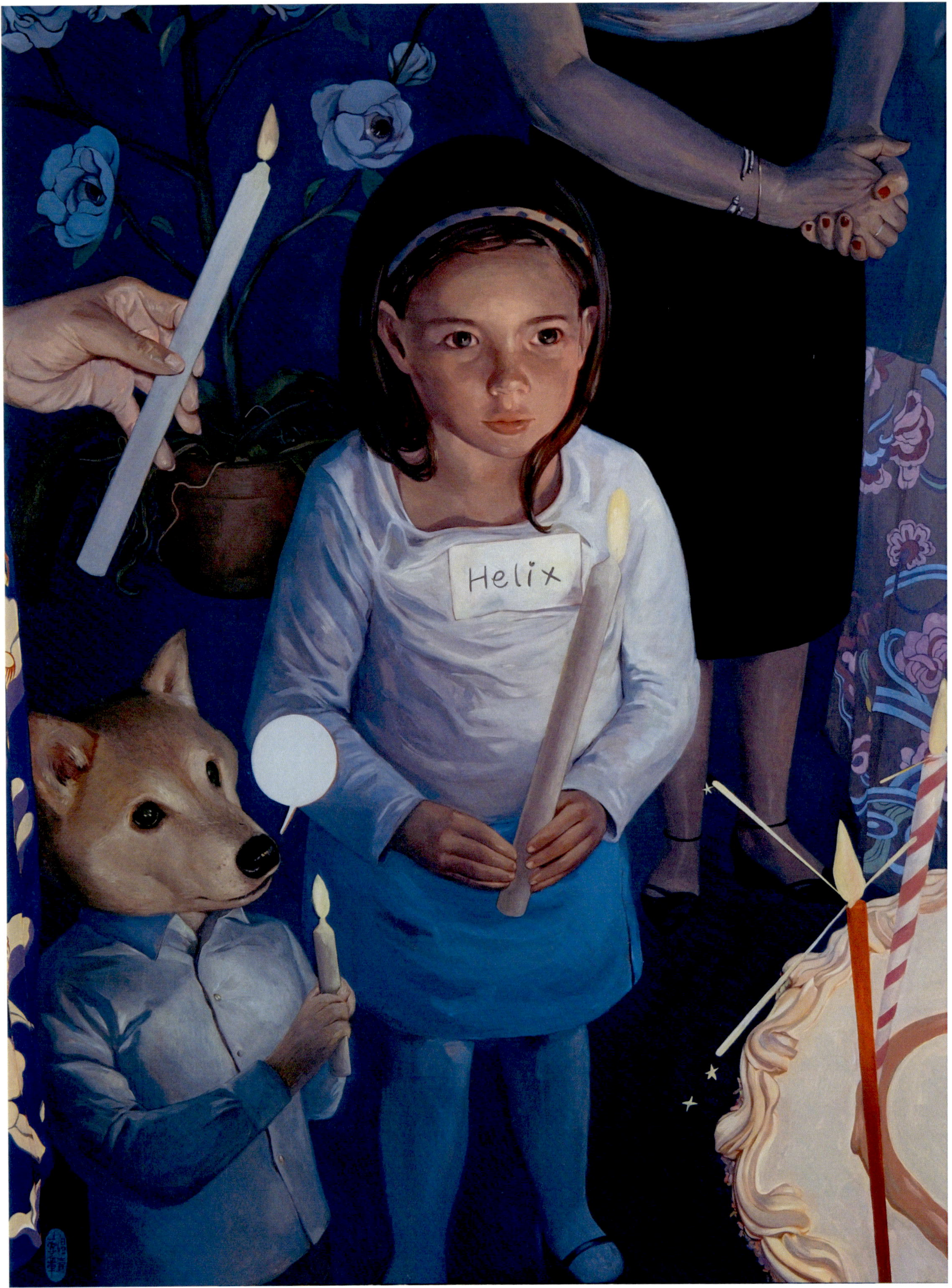
Helix

Preludes

Helice Wen

September 8-29
2018

Spoke Art San Francisco is pleased to present **Preludes**, a solo exhibition by San Francisco-based artist **Helice Wen**. For her second solo exhibition with the gallery, Wen will exhibit new drawings, paintings and photographs exploring the patterns of everyday life.

"In music, the prelude is an introductory piece; the smaller motif that will appear repeatedly through the whole act," Helice Wen explains. Creating a visual prelude, Wen introduces the viewer to patterns throughout her everyday life. From the wink of a candle to the unfurling of a flower and its eventual death, the artist explores the beauty of these small, fleeting moments that can be overlooked.

Incorporating her traditional training in Chinese watercolor and calligraphy, Wen's work displays both a tightly controlled command of her medium alongside fluid and serendipitous mark making. Exhibiting her photographs for the first time, we are given a behind the scenes view into Wen's artistic process. The artist's widely varied practice from carefully photographing her subjects to delicate drawings and richly colored paintings offer the viewer a small glimpse into intimate moments and recollections of memories.

Helice Wen

Cake (May All Your Wishes Come True) (detail)
oil on panel
36" x 36" (2018)

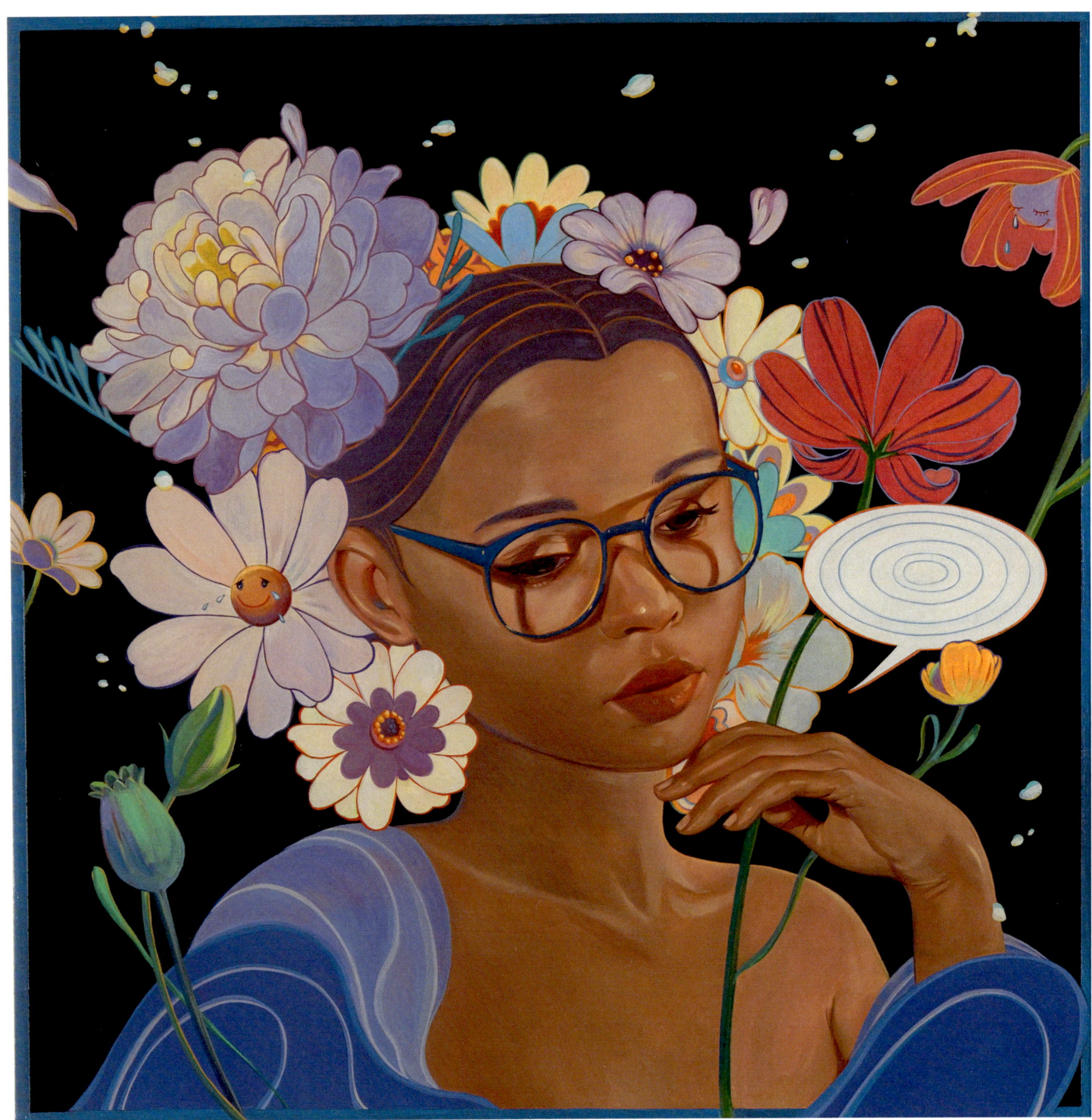

Helice Wen

Sweetness No. 5

acrylic and oil on wood panel
20˝ x 20˝ (2018)

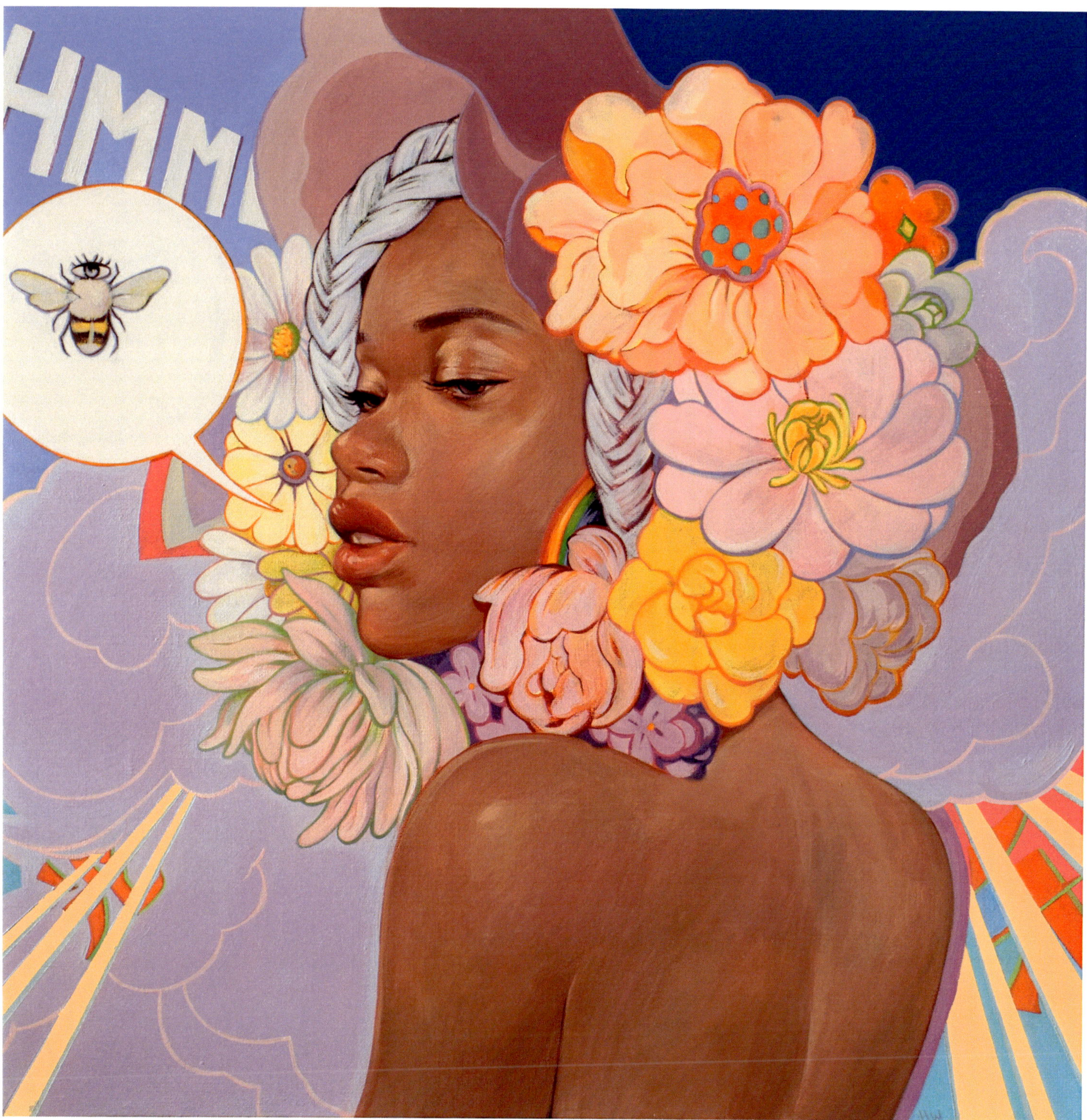

Sweetness No. 4
acrylic on canvas
24˝ x 24˝ (2018)

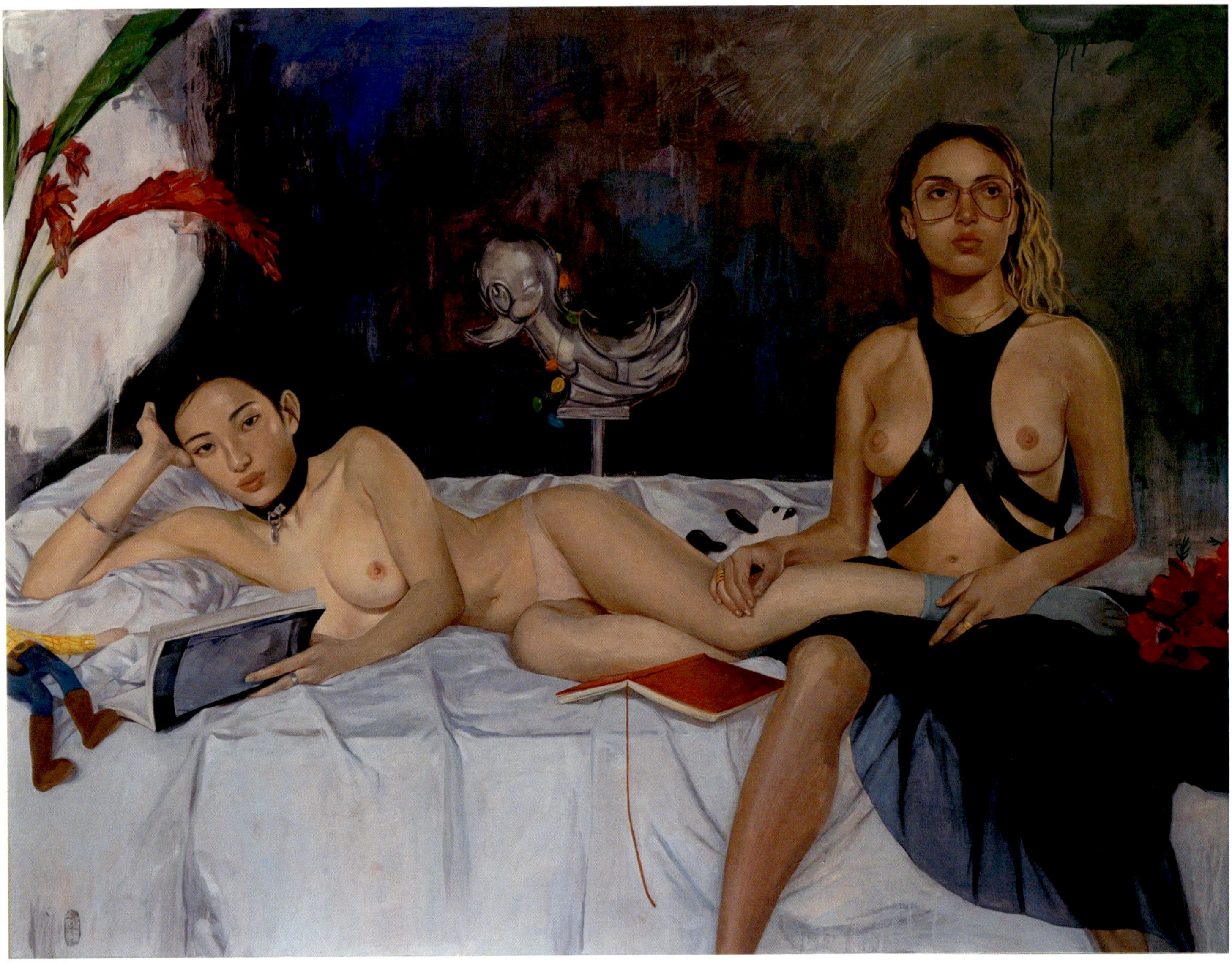

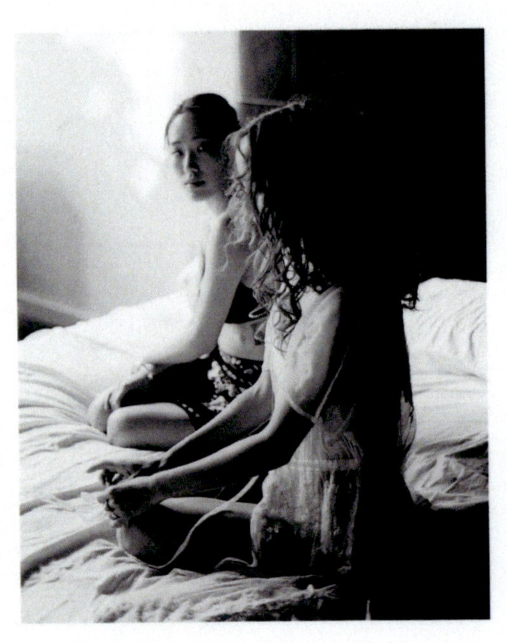

A. *Helice Wen*
Woven
oil on panel
36" x 48" (2018)

B. *Helice Wen*
Photo No. 2
polaroid
3½" x 4¼" (2018)

C. *Helice Wen*
Motif
graphite, sumi ink, water color,
acrylic, gold foil on paper
22" x 30½" (2018)

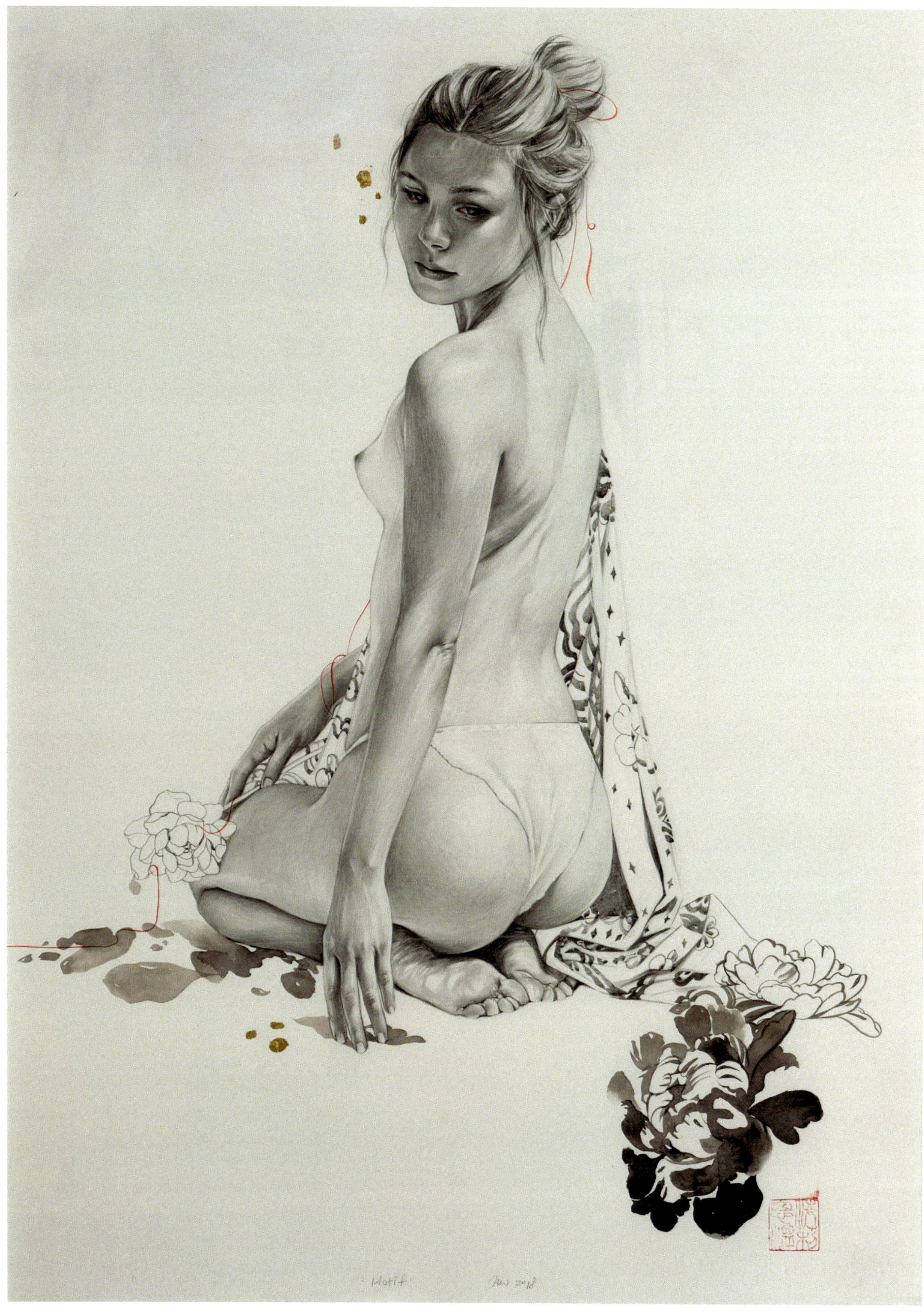

C.

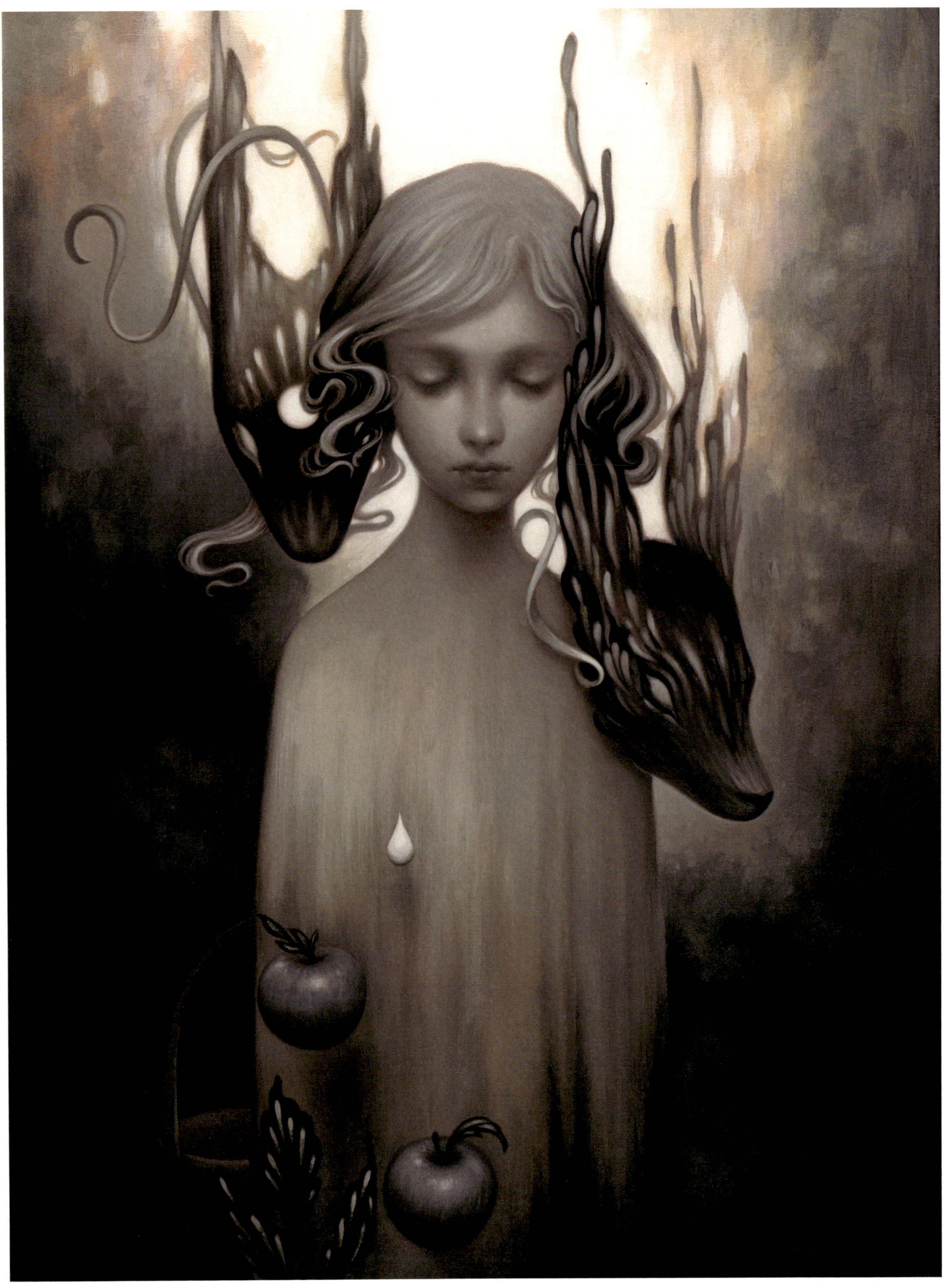

Lore

Amy Sol

October 6—27
2018

Spoke Art San Francisco is pleased to present *Lore*, a solo exhibition by Bay Area-based artist *Amy Sol*. For her first solo exhibition with the gallery, Sol will exhibit ethereal new paintings and sculptures expounding on her mythological visual language.

Exploring how nature and femininity intersect, Sol's figures are elegant and serene with a stoic, introspective power. Both her sculptural work and oil paintings are frozen scenes taken from airy dreams and tales.

Incorporating traditional oil painting and sculpting techniques as well as virtual reality and 3D printing, Sol has masterfully blended mediums to explore light, atmosphere, dimensionality and mood in this new body of work. Characters and figures are rendered both in graceful oil paintings and dynamic sculptural works utilizing digital- based and classic tools to create a visual language all her own.

Amy Sol
Before Nightfall
oil on panel
12˝ x 16˝ (2018)

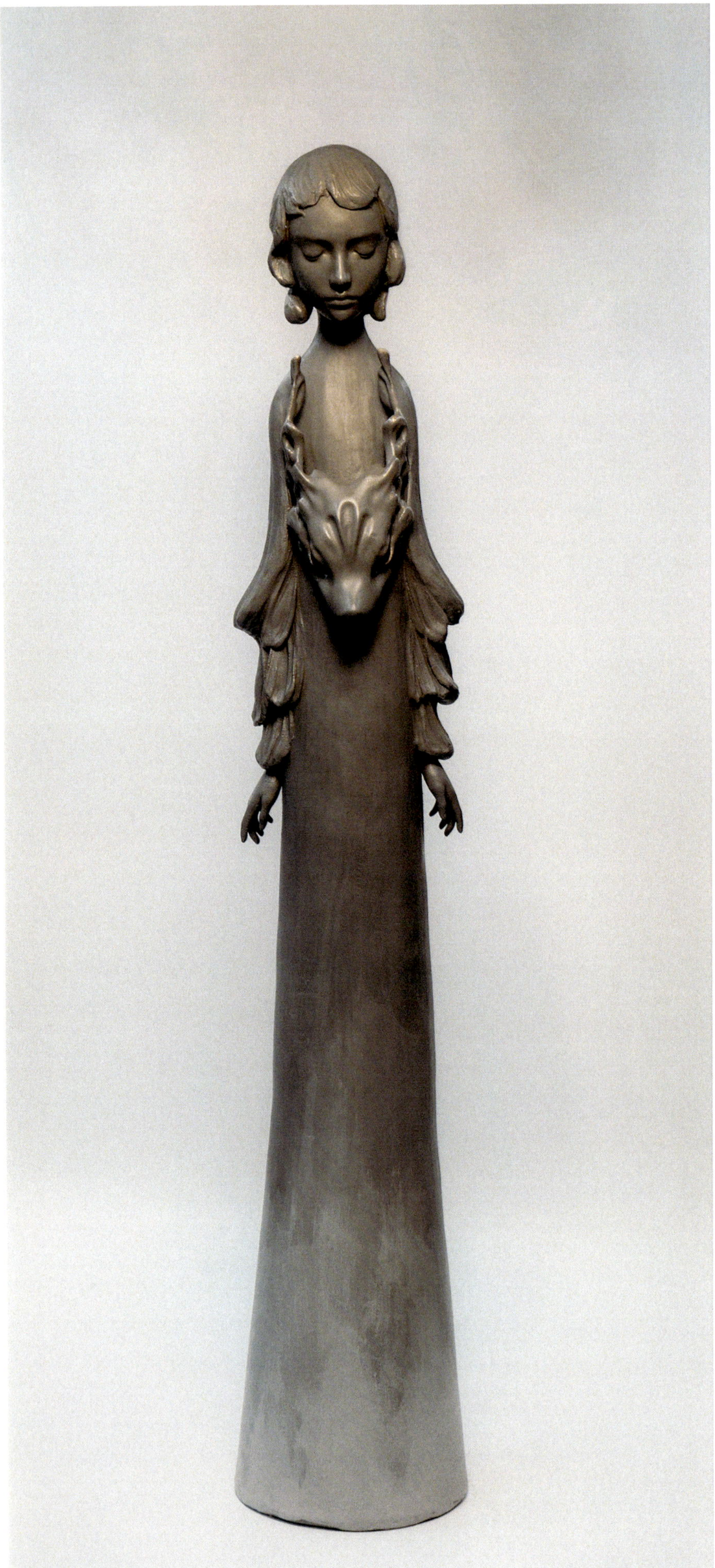

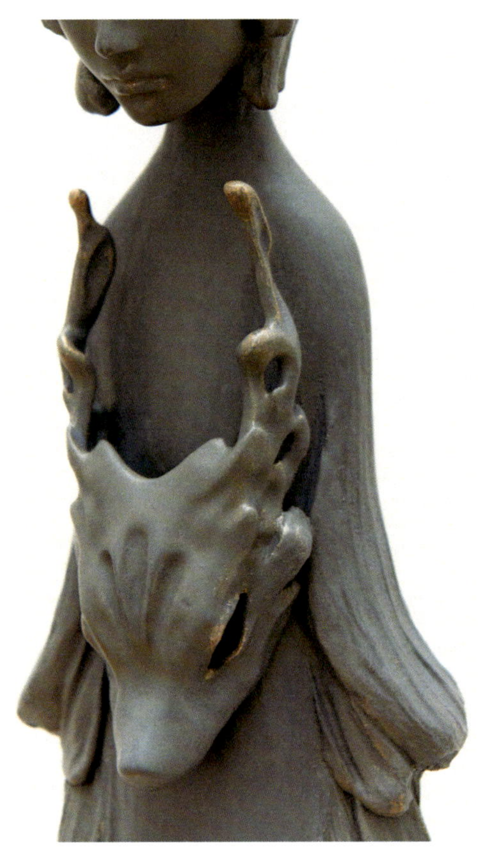

Rhymes Shadow

resin, enamel and oil paint

4" x 21" (2018)

Vespers Dream

resin, enamel and oil paint
5" x 22" (2018)

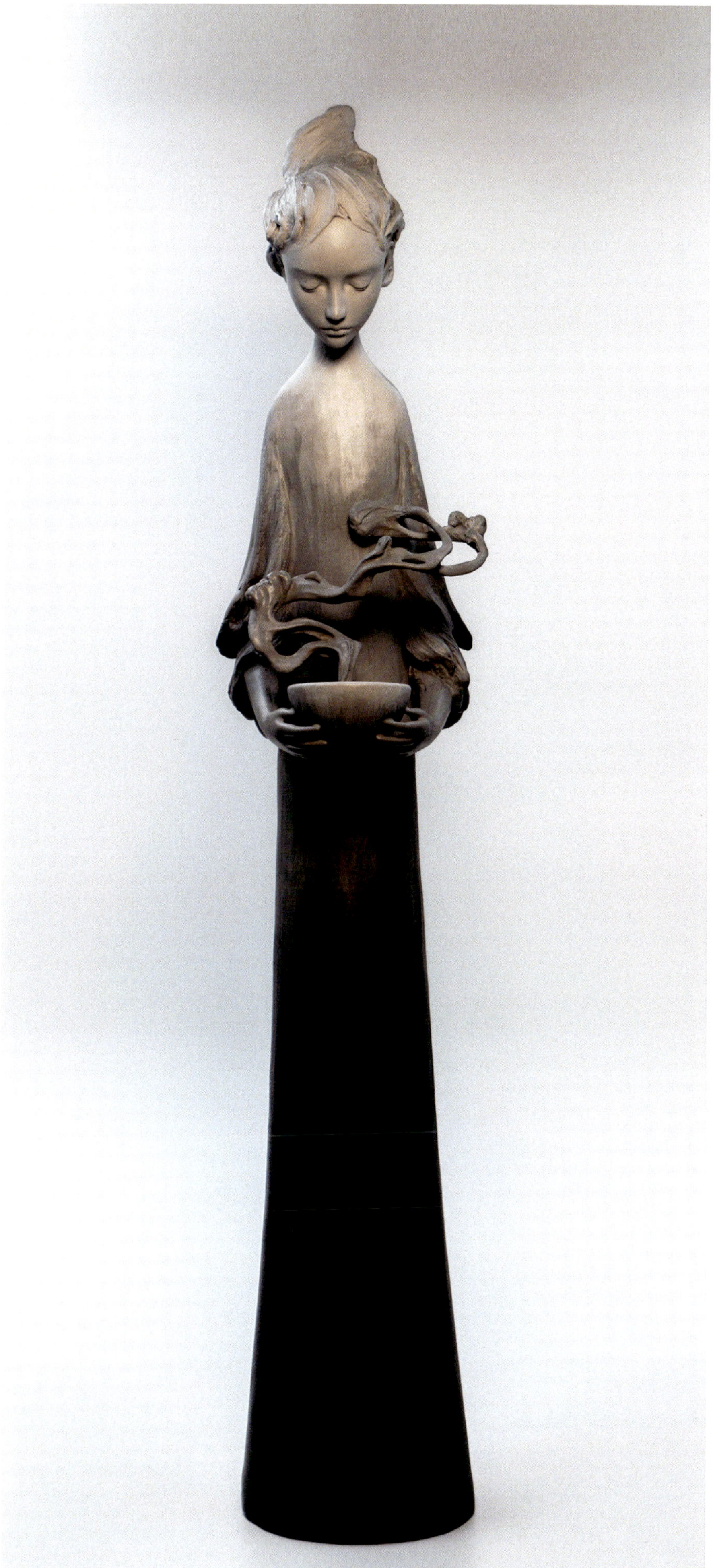

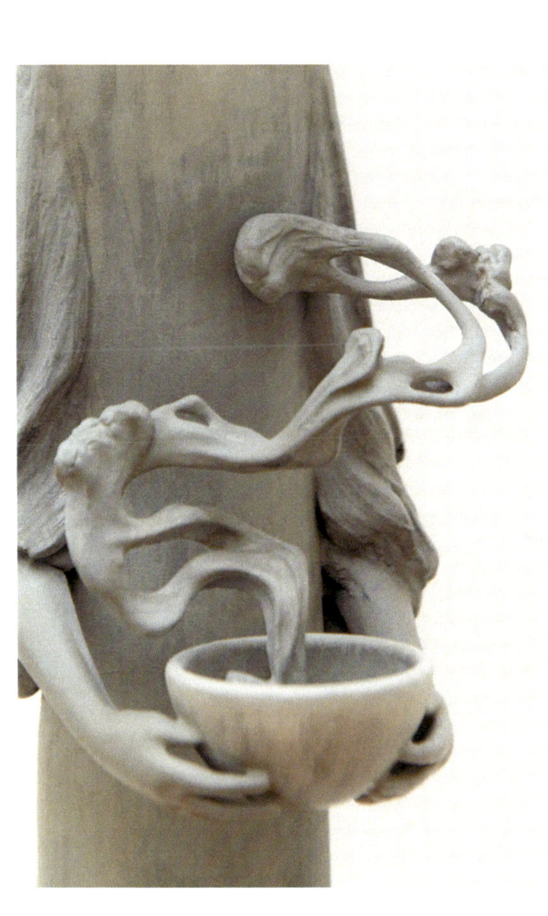

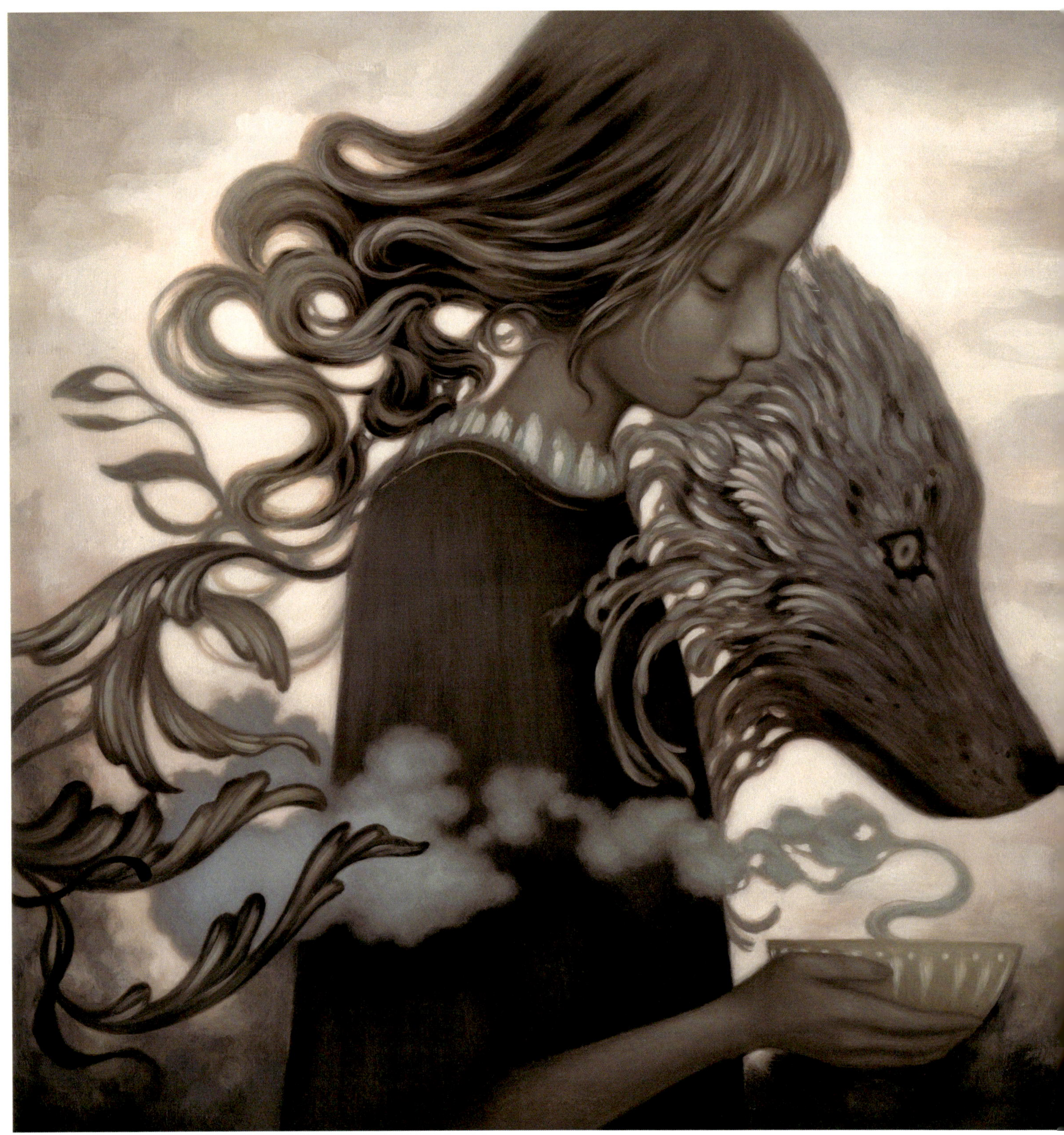

Amy Sol
Evening Air
oil on panel
12" x 16" (2018)

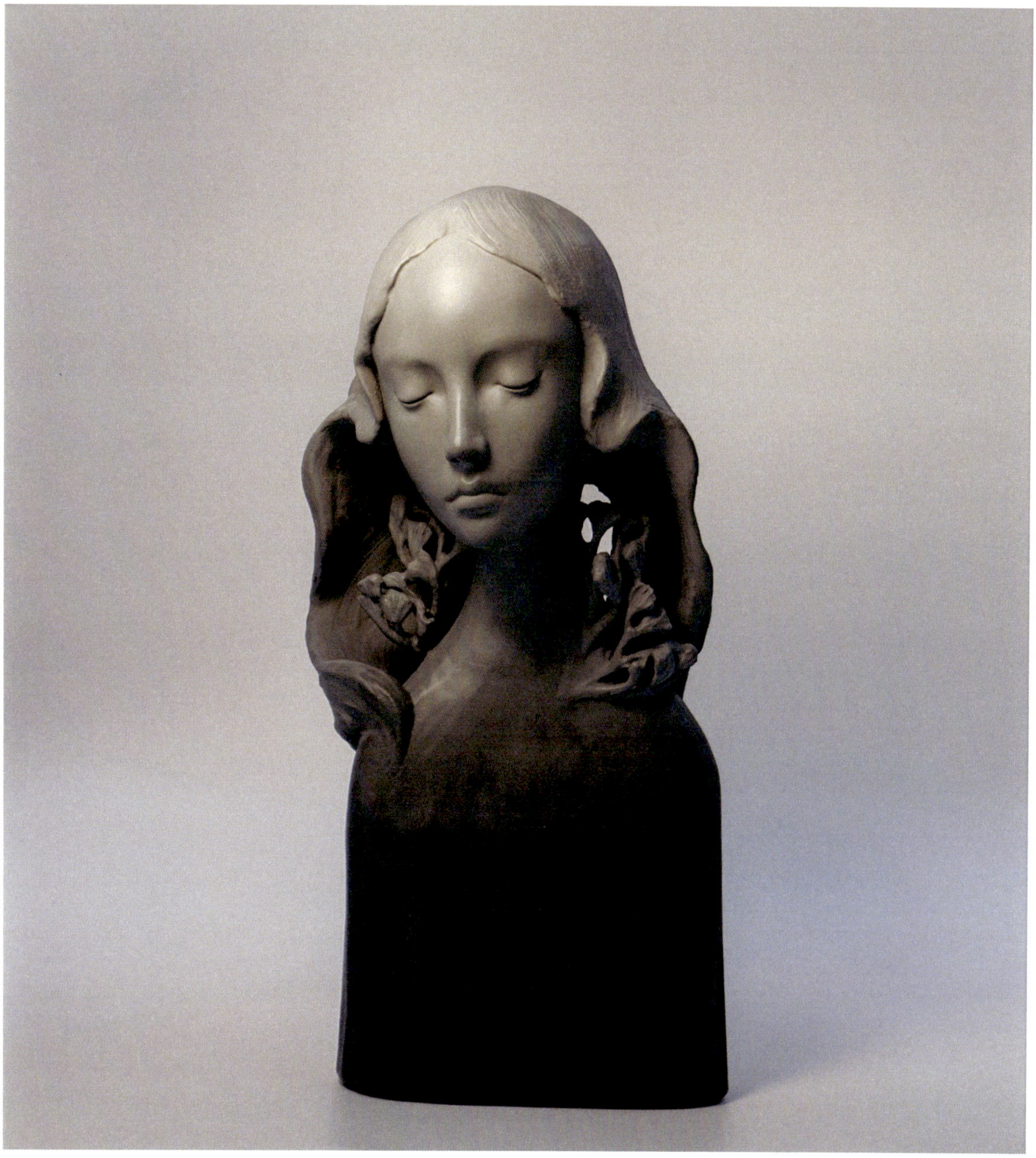

Amy Sol

Rae
resin, enamel and oil paint
6" x 12" (2018)

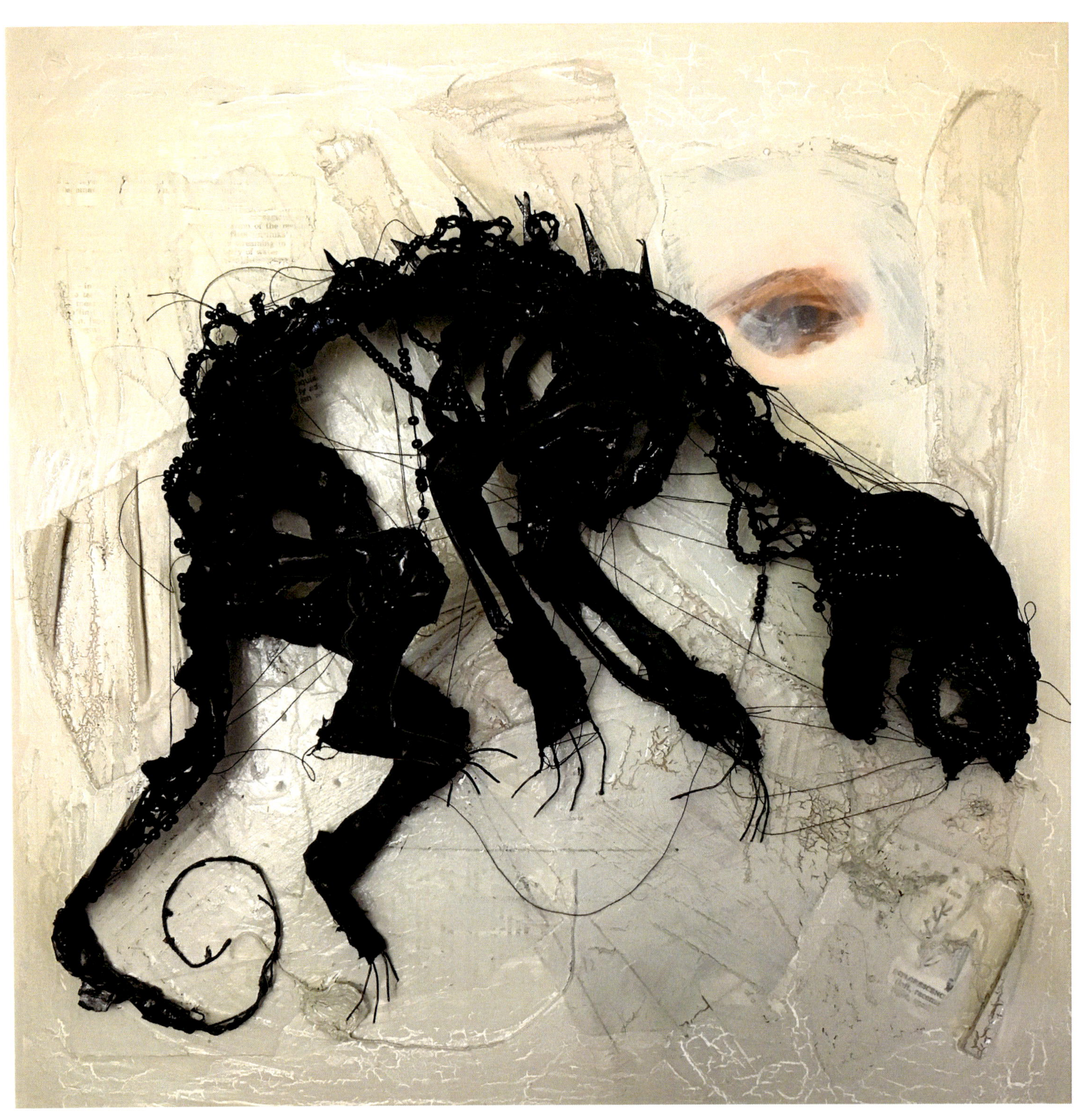

A Werewolf of Truly
Demonical Ferocity

mixed media
12" x 12" x 4½" (2018)

Fantasia

A Group Exhibition curated by Paintguide

November 3—17
2018

Spoke Art is pleased to present *Fantasia*, a group exhibition curated by *Paintguide* featuring over 40 international artists from around the world. This dynamic group exhibition brings together artists from the online community formed around the hugely popular Instagram account into the physical gallery space.

In music, "fantasia" refers to a composition incorporating different styles, which are often improvised. Artists were given creative freedom with only one restriction, keep the work within a 12 x 12 inch space. The dimensional uniformity mirrors the presentation of images on Instagram where artworks must grab the viewer's attention without the hubris of size, context and setting.

The online platform's influence on art through wide dissemination is undeniable. Teddy Chan, Creative Director of Paintguide and exhibition curator, cites Walter Benjamin's 'The Work of Art in the Mechanical Age of Reproduction', *"the near-perfect reproducibility of images in the modern age diminishes the artwork's 'aura' or unique presence in time and space. This emancipates art from the religious or private hierarchies that often determine our response to the work."* The communalization of imagery poses challenges in viewers increasingly limited attention or contemplation of artworks. Paintguide strives to create a virtual salon, providing space for conversations and the sharing of ideas.

Participating Artists:

Ali Cavanaugh • Christopher Charles Curtis • Jun Chen Yan • AM DeBrincat • Johan Deckmann • Florian Eymann • Simon Fensholm • Jayde Fish • Eric Fok • Erik Formoe • Felicia Forte • Alexandra Gallagher • Lola Gil • Jessica Hess • Hidden Velvet • Erik Jones • Jang Koal • Fabio La Fauci • Joey Leung • Linsey Lvendall • Lorraine Loots • Guillermo Lorca GH • Daniel Martin • Rui Matsunaga • Caitlin T. Mc Cormack • Miss Van • Victor Montahini • Nadezda • Daniel Ochoa • Karla Ortiz • Reisha Perlmutter • Flavia Pitis • Michael Reeder • Erika Sanada • Elly Smallwood • Jessica So Ren Tang • Loribelle Spirovoski • Roos van der Vliet • Emilio Villalba • Helice Wen • John Wentz • Vincent Xeus • Yoskay Yamamoto

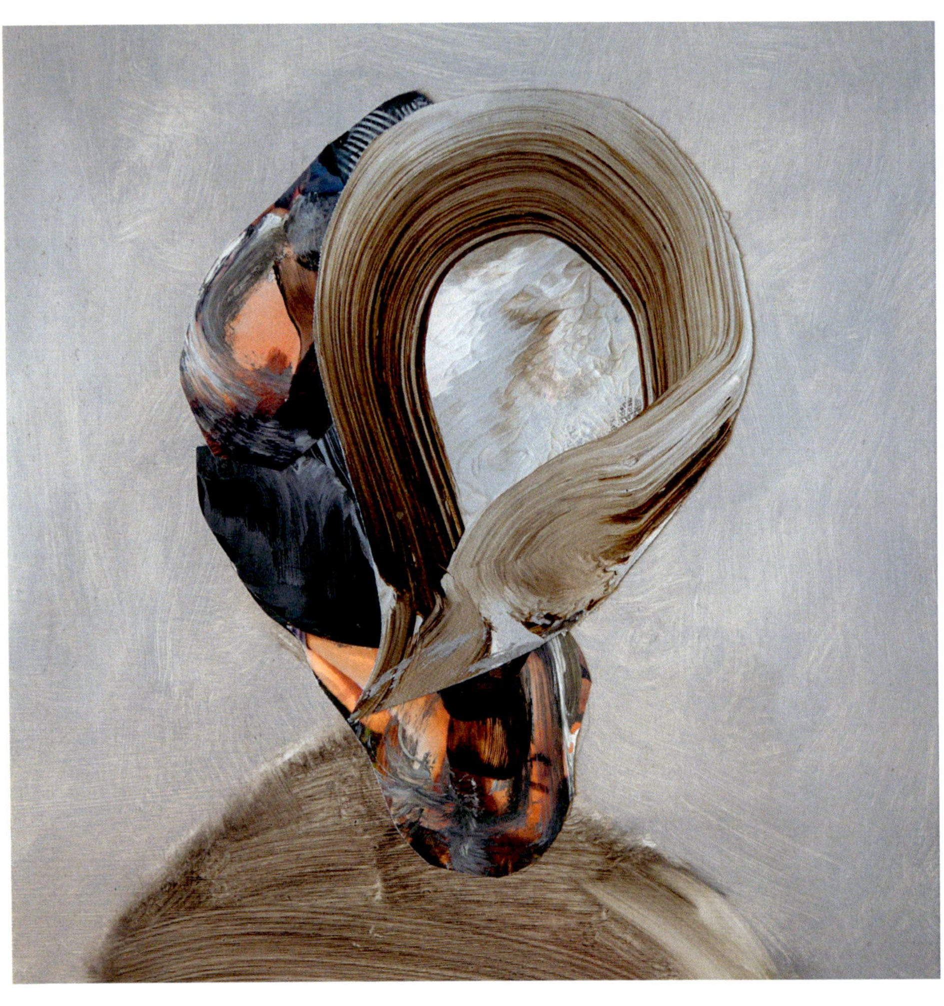

Daniel Martin
Study VII (2018),
Morphos Series
oil and acrylic collage mounted on panel
12˝ x 12˝ (2018)

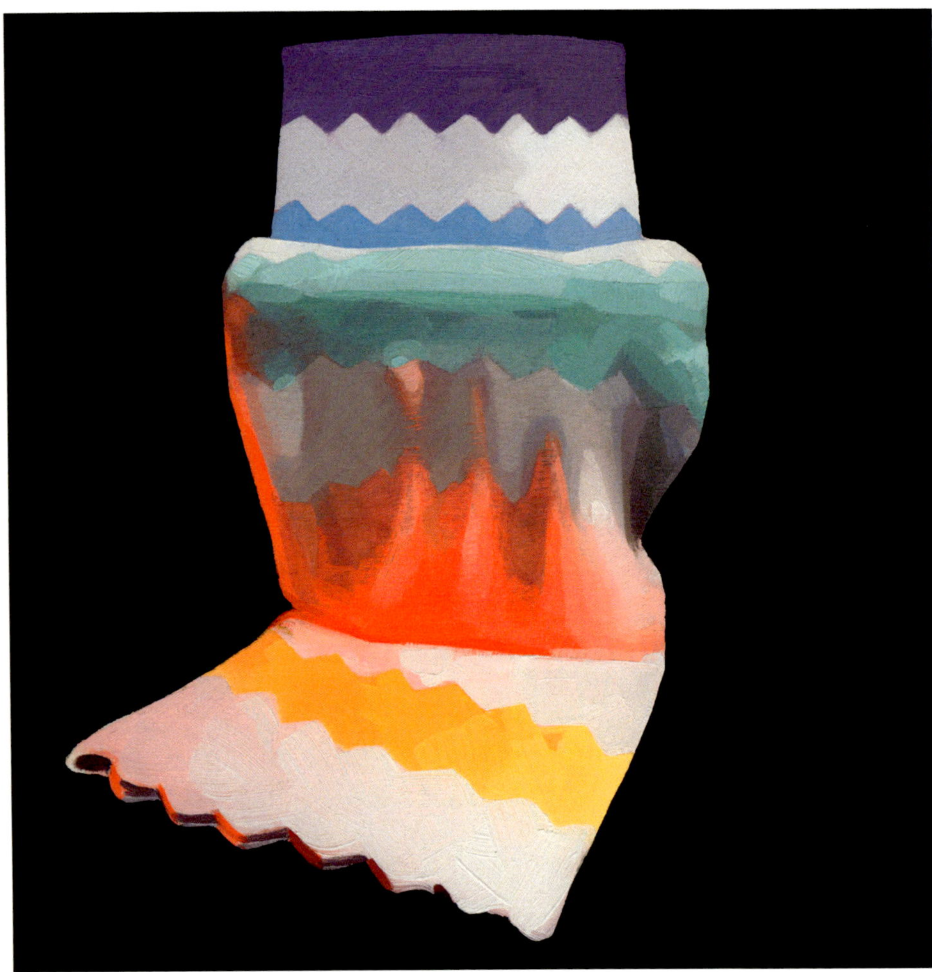

Felicia Forte
Afghan Abstracted-
Black No.2
oil on archival paper
12˝ x 12˝ (2018)

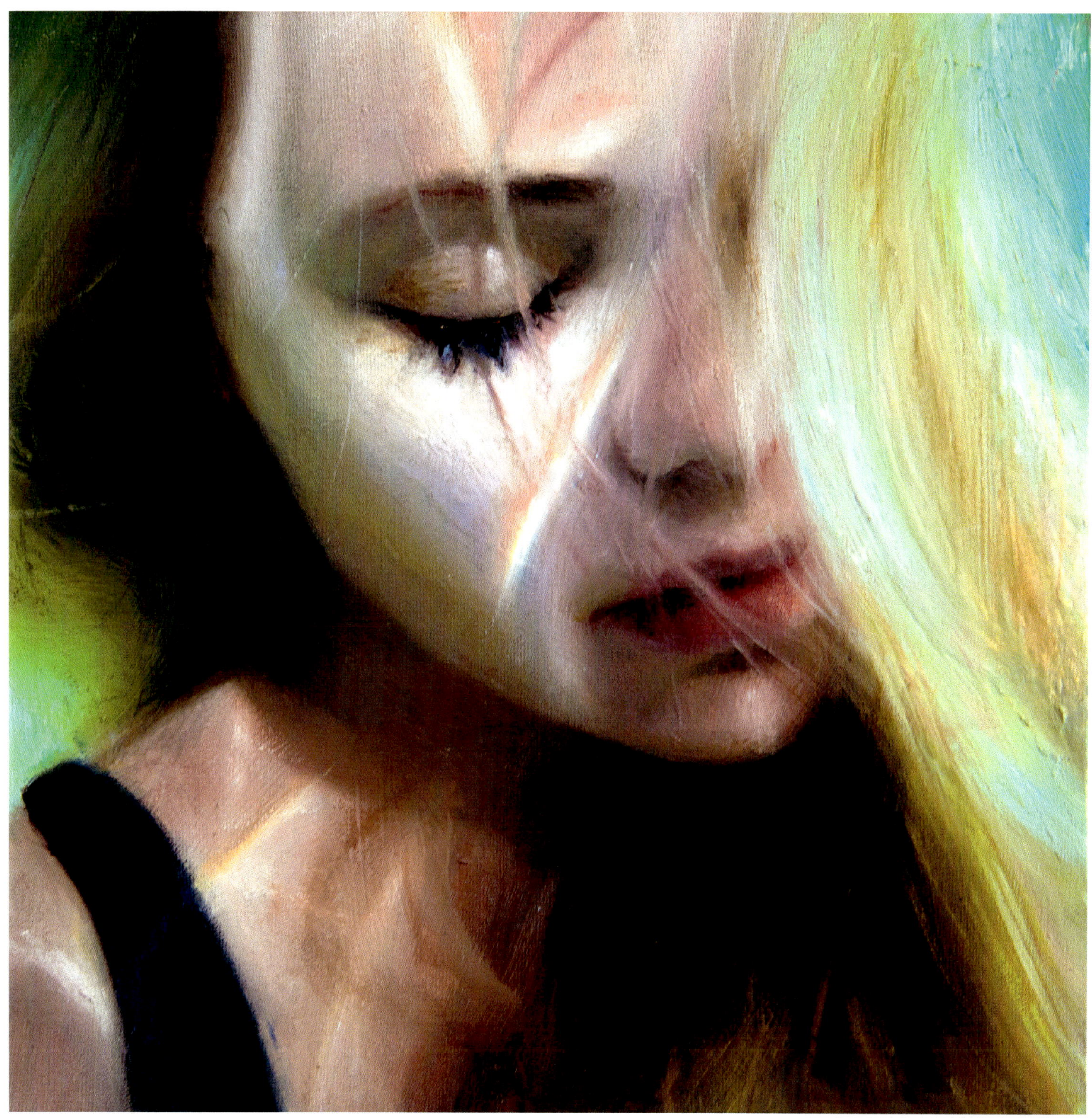

Reisha Perlmutter

Pluto

oil on canvas
12˝ x 12˝ (2018)

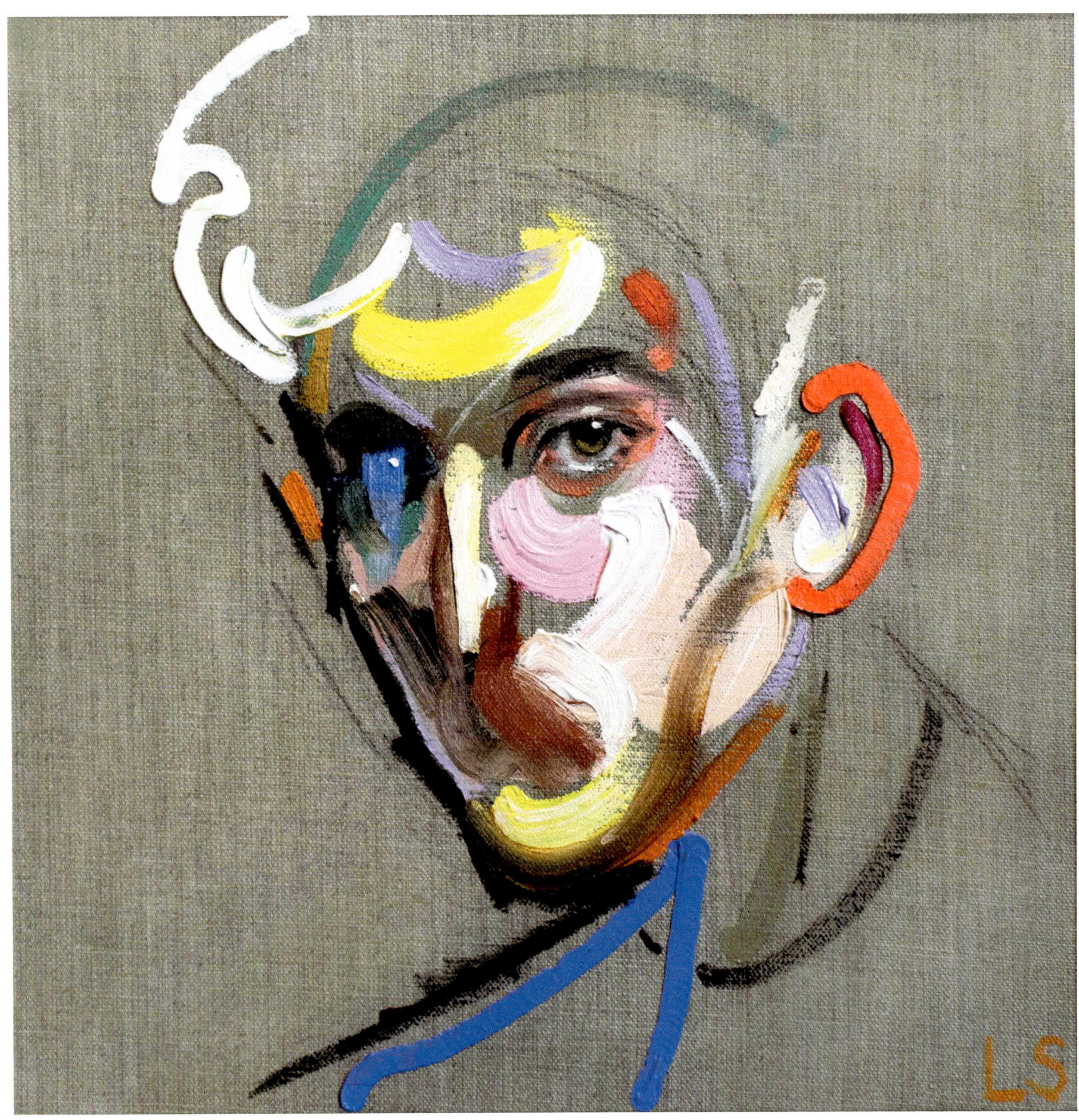

Loribelle Spirovski
Homme 94
oil on linen
12˝ x 12˝ (2018)

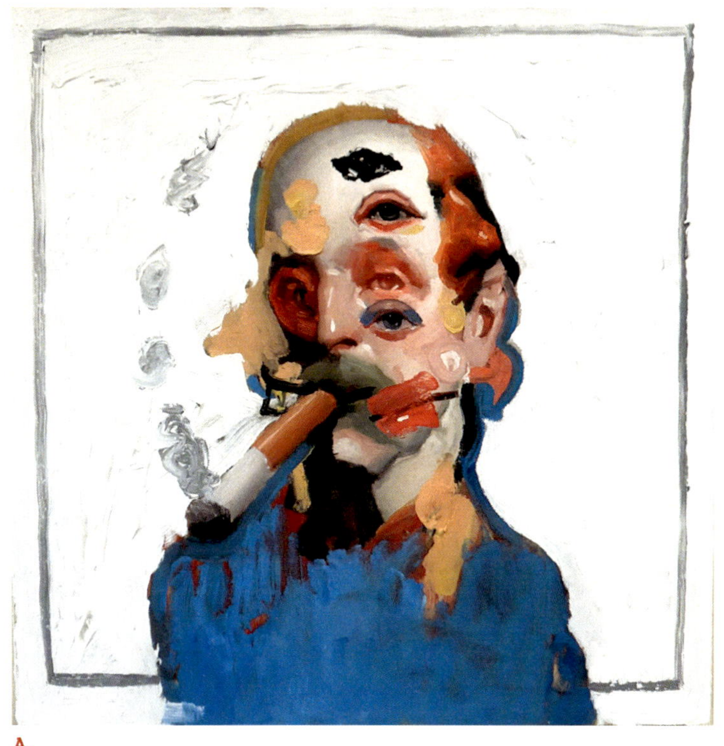

A.

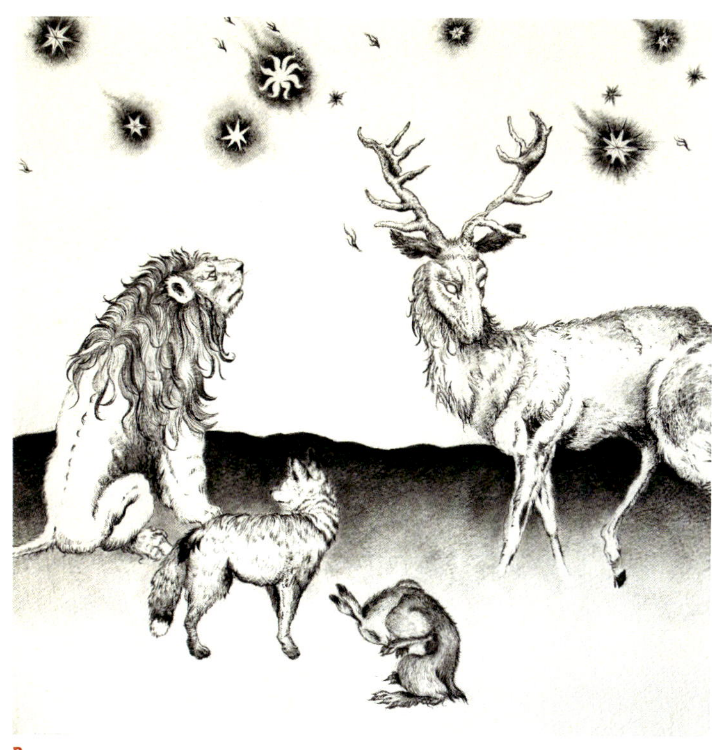

B.

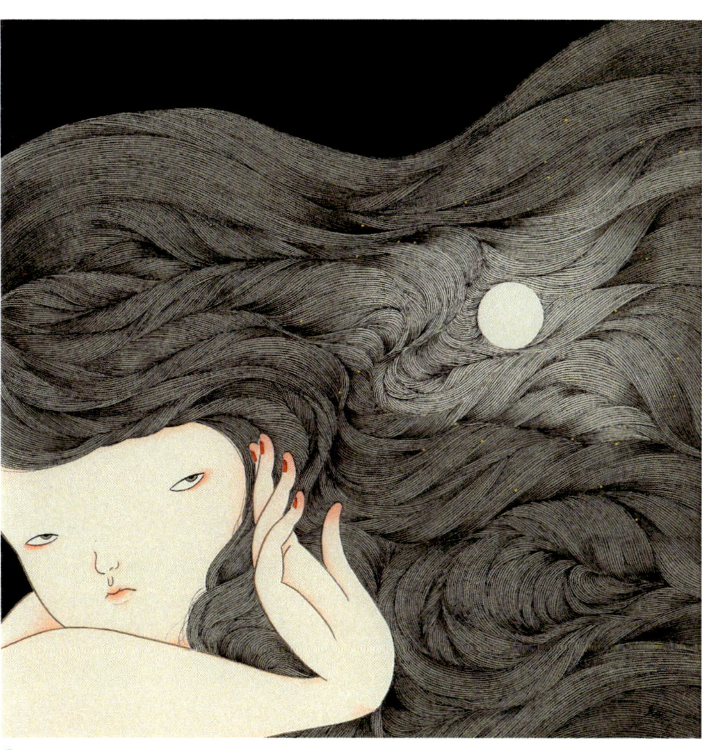

C.

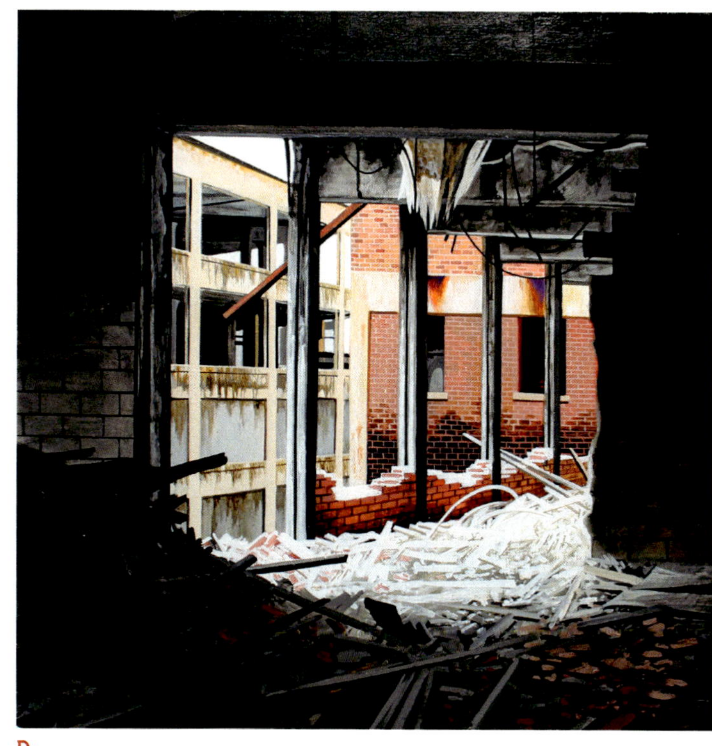

D.

A. *Emilio Villalba*

Smoking Sarge

oil on wood

12˝ x 12˝ (2018)

B. *Rui Matsunaga*

Underneath the Sky That's Ever Falling Down

ink on paper

12˝ x 12˝ (2018)

C. *Joey Leung*

Catch the Moon

Chinese ink, gouache, ink pen, acrylic, coloured pencil on rice paper

12˝ x 12˝ (2018)

D. *Jessica Hess*

Detritus I

acrylic on panel

12˝ x 12˝ (2018)

About Spoke

SPOKE is an art space specializing in new contemporary painting, sculpture and illustration with an emphasis in accessible programming. Started in 2010, the gallery now houses two locations, one in San Francisco's Lower Nob Hill neighborhood and one in New York City's Lower East Side. Each space rotates monthly exhibits that feature a wide variety of solo and group shows, many of which feature an international roster of represented artists.

Throughout the year we also do pop-up shows, conventions and art fairs around the country and you can usually find us in New York, Chicago, Los Angeles or Miami at least once a year.

Spoke Art is a DBA of Harman Hashimoto Enterprises LLC.

Spoke Art SF
816 Sutter Street
San Francisco, CA 94109

+1.415.796.3774
SF@spoke-art.com

Spoke Art NYC
210 Rivington Street
New York, NY 10002

+1.212.477.4759
NYC@spoke-art.com

www.spoke-art.com

Colophon

The Spoke Art San Francisco Annual 2018 was designed in San Francisco, California by *Shaun Roberts*. The book was printed and bound in the United States by *Edition One* on Super Smooth Uncoated 100lb text weight (148gsm) paper using PUR adhesive. The type was composed using the *Odudo* & *Odudo Slab* font families by *Thom Niessink*.

Second printing.
March, 2019

© 2018 *Paragon Books*. All rights reserved. This book or any portion thereof may not be reproduced or used in any manner whatsoever without the express written permission of the publisher except for the use of brief quotations in a book review.

ISBN: 978-1-7327980-2-1

Introduction © 2018 *Dasha Matsuura*, used with permission.

Opening Reception Images (pp. 9, 14–15, 29, & 47), Installation View Images (pp. 28, 32–33) © 2018 *Shaun Roberts*, used with permission.

$25.00
ISBN 978-1-7327980-2-1
52500

9 781732 798021

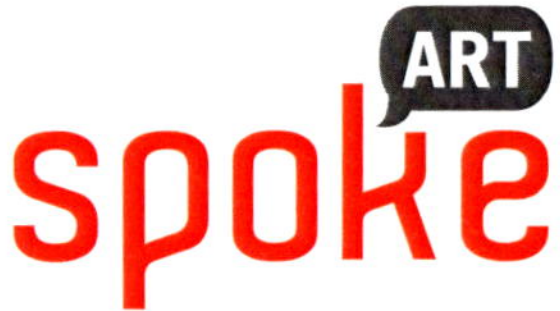